Sovereign Covenant
"Without Prejudice" UCC 1-207

By

William Dixon

First Amendment Study Team is purely educational and informative in nature and does not constitute professional, legal or illegal tax advice.

ISBN: 978-1-4140-1735-8 (sc)
ISBN: 978-1-4140-1734-1 (e)

Print information available on the last page.

This book is printed on acid-free paper.

1stBooks - rev. 09/11/2020

Author's Internet web site: God Is Sovereign First Amendment Study Team
http://godissovereignfast.com/

TABLE OF CONTENTS

Chapter 1: In Propria Persona

Propria Persona: Silk Purse v. sow's ear: in personam.

God's Republic plays "Public Law" and is Thee Sovereign Silk Purse. Democratic 'public policy' plays the part of the sow's ear at 'engrafted' contract, with a couple of wiggly tails as 'devise,' no police power pun intended. No actual pig's wiggly or silk purses were at 'action' in this treatise. The old Dragon however, must covet its many lobes or lose her entirety to Truth.

This treatise does not contain fancy words, only the tongue of the "serpent" and to be "as wise" you must Know it, for the words are soothing to the old Dragon's lobes and your Grace is Peace. This information is Scribe of Black's Law 5th Edition and Thee King James Bible.

Personam is your individual God given silk purse, as free as your Creation. You give up your silk purse each time you sign an agency sow's ear contract, because you waive another contract, Thee Bill of Rights and New Covenant. I have all my purses in silk; mine are just dirtier than yours should be. You will be collecting many ears as you stutter through this material, and it is my prayer that all your Covenants are silk purses with pearls.

To become 'subject' and 'made liable' to Article I Legislated and Article II Executor/Admiralty is as easy as signing your children into pre-school. Enrollment office will show our proud flag, Admiralty. The signing of the corporate birth certificate, the Child's assignment of SS#, is where the birthright switch is made from "entitled" Rights to 'subject' civil Liberties. Under the Common Law a parent may contract a Child's name to an instrument, seeking faith and fairness, but agency has not the power. This activity does not take much practice because we sign contracts all the time. The W-4 instrument was by far the best Dragon lobe I ever pinched, because it was the most obvious and worrisome 'devise.'

"Without Prejudice" UCC 1-207 above your signature will reserve your Rights. Police activity cannot dissuade Personam to switch loyalty in the schoolyard to in personam and 'thing in action.'

The sow's ear is obtained by signing negotiable units unconditionally, thereby triggering the police power of agency. The winged Serpent

"Penumbra" has 'engrafted' the Separation of Powers at the Voting House of Article I and the War Wagon of Article II, which makes and enforces the sow's ear unit for your "benefit." Article III and Thee Bill of Rights are the only conquest left for the many headed Beast and Penumbra is diverting Lady Justice with "engraft" of law and 'devise.'

Black's Law 5th. Personal jurisdiction. The power of a court over the person of a defendant in contrast to the jurisdiction of a court over a defendant's property or his interest therein; in personam as opposed to in rem jurisdiction.

A state citizen is born with silk purse personam and becomes in personam and actionable to recover money after signing an 'unconditional' agreement with the Article I sow's ear agency.

Rights are inalienable within Thee Bill of Rights and Article III Judiciary, but seldom 'prayed' for lack of knowledge. Natural Law Rights cannot be taken away, but may be waived by contractual 'devise,' because agency does not have police power over the state Citizen without assent and nexus. Without force being applied we give police agency permission to send corporate officers to our homes and schoolyard by contract, which are "unconditional" Maritime requirements at Rule 12. (b).

Jurisdiction over your "personam" requires assent by 'devise' so we do not wiggle. Subsequently agency units, contracts with police power of 14th Amendment 'due process' to 'gang sweep,' 'profile' and declare state Citizens "persons' of interest," and charter agency to take your pet ferret. Statutes charter agency 'makes' police power to issue 'obligation' 'certificates,' which are 'negotiable' in the sow's ear Tribunal. W-4 is such an instrument, as is bank accounts, presentments, selective service, jury duty summons, and drivers' license and school enrollment. These are only a few of the many heads of the statute Beast "Penumbra Doctrine."

Black's Law 5th. Penumbra Doctrine. The implied powers of the federal government predicated on the necessary and Proper Clause of the U.S. Const., Art. I Sec. 8 (18) permits one implied power to be engrafted on another implied power. Kohl v. U.S., 91 U.S. 367, 23 L.Ed. 449.

Article I and Article II Implied power have no foundation without the un-Implied Power of Article III Judiciary and none have the power to 'permit' the Separation of Powers to 'engraft' other implied powers. We Thee People give that power at signature assent and thereby contract our silk purse state Sovereign "personam," to in personam U.S. Citizen at "domestic product" "action."

Congress gave us the choice, as God does, and we contracted our children into 'forum' public schools. Article I Legislative is firmly 'engrafted' to Article II Executive/Admiralty. The 'devise' are 'unconditional' 'negotiable instruments' signed by you and executed by Executive/Maritime Law and sister Heads of Penumbra 'inferior' Tribunals that brings police power to the schoolyard by contract.

We collect the 'engraft' sow's ear by agency fiat of 'unconscionable' contract, license, and enrollments. The signing at UCC 3-104.1, which if "unconditional" at UCC 3-104.2 gives agency police power to access your property by executing negotiable "dishonored" instruments of "promise" per UCC 3-104.3. This power does not extent to the shopping mall, because not all Citizens are contracted in the same permissive manner and street citizens wiggle more than contracted children with parental consent to use "public policy," as protective 'devise.'

No Citizen may sign an 'unconditional promise' without waiving Rights and becoming in personam to actions of non criminal issue. 'Without prejudice' UCC 1-207 turns the sow's ear instrument into a silk purse for the state Citizen, because all Rights are reserved and in personam is restored to personam. A resident alien gets the sow's ear whether he wants it or not. He must assent to his master, as we must Obey God. God's silk purse has the Choice. We must give credit to 'civil' Law of man at Article I and use our 'reserved' rights to God's Judicial law of Article III and Separation of Powers to complete our work via Acts 22:25 and avoid Article II altogether.

A "centurion" agent is on "Notice" that his jurisdiction extends to criminal matters only and teaching Truth is not an "enabling cause" for police power. "Probable cause" must be at action against Paul of Tarsus, who was a "natural born Citizen" Art. 2, Sec 1, Cl. 5, of Rome. Today his Plea of Sovereign Covenant is called Habeas Corpus. We Thee People have this great power to defeat the same inferior and presumptuous adversary. A crime requires the judgment of man based on God's Law. If the State is harmed without victim, then Caesar is obvious with his elliptical manner and the tithes he seeks are not his. Judgment in a 'competent' court of jurisdiction must reflect Truth. Knowledge of Law will assure Grace.

A Grand Jury may summon a state Citizen with Police Power, which begins at 'probable' cause. A U.S. Citizen may be "held" by 'devise' of 'reasonable cause.' An 'action' in personam is statute and has no power over a silk purse, only the implied sow's ear of agency and no competent counsel is found therein. The administrative record of 'inferior' Tribunal in 'corporate America' 'must' be 'unconditional' in personam to 'promise' and must be Maritime in nature of contract. 'Navagatable waters' take on a different meaning when on the 'highway' 'cruisers' violate the state Citizen's Right to free intercourse, by turning Liberty into license of sow's ear 'devise.'

God intended us to care for others and knowledgeable operators of equipment are very necessary. We also must have insurance to protect our brother from errant behavior and accident. All I want to do is blend with the sow's ears, not become one. We state Citizens are not corporate until we sign the corporate license. I sign as a silk purse and agency cannot get confused or their interference is actionable under 'color of Law' statutes of Title 18.

In Personam enlistment and swearing perjury oath in ignorance is voidable, but YOU must rebut each agency individually, selective service may reappear and you can rebut the presumption of 'subject' Citizenship. Enlistment requirements are the same as a negotiable W-4, merely sign unconditionally and it is a done deal, up to and including the "promise" at UCC 3-104.3 and "scourging." The state Citizen is not 'made liable' until signature upon an 'unconditional' instrument at UCC 3-104.2. The best way is to write on the face of the enrollments or prima facie, Thee Reservation of Rights on the unit prior to signing it. You make agency wiggle that tail whilst it has it. Agent may also object to further violation of his "unconditional" instrument being conditioned and snatch it from you. Knowing Thee Truth will make you "meek" and therefore not humbled. Cooperate with agency officers and sign all documents with Your Silk Purse personam intact, your Spirit will not worry.

If I were Alpha wolf and you were Omega wolf: all you would have to do is roll over on your back, let me nip you in a couple of my favorite places, don't dare bite me and I'll only 'make action,' and I won't nip you to hard unless you try to wiggle, defend yourself, or spray me.

This is why US "sheep" are alpha to the omega wolf. Truth stands the middle of the two with shepherd's staff of authority. Jesus has allowed my pasture with the wolf, only because I am very humbly as wise as the serpent. News from the front is very promising, MPs everywhere, if only there were a few more sheep up here.

A petition of 'persons' will only 'give' what Congress legislates as civil rights; a lot of sow's ear contracts, simmering in the old Dragon's milk of Admiralty. You must not waive Rights, neither may you be forced to sign any document without intention; you must do so willingly, and with full knowledge and understanding of its content. If contracts are signed under fraud, duress or 'devise,' such are void ab initio. With 'revocation' of signature, on Maritime Instruments especially, abates police power and thereby jurisdiction over non U.S. Citizens. Department of Justice is not Article III Judiciary, and is "inferior" to state Law at Calif. Code 22.2.

Negotiable Instruments Law requires the same statute "must" as Maritime contract and begins with W-4, 'enlistment,' 'public school registry," HMO or banking and employment insurance and activation clause for use of police power. Personam signature to an "unconditional" agreement at UCC 3-104.2, while vital to the Military, is 'unconscionable' to the silk purse of the state Citizen. In personam gives agency possession and permission to police your default or dishonor to subject matter tribunal. We Thee People who sign 'unconditional' agreements leave the silk purse open to the same Choice, mischief of Admiralty 'subject matter' only court. After signature you have no freedom of Choice until you personally void the instrument. Agency is the 'cruiser' of choice for Admiralty, for the sow's ear cannot admit its 'engrafted' police power upon the silk purse. Instead fraudulent license 'devise' is used as presumed mandate to action force, until rebutted.

Legislative Acts are Sister 'implied powers' at 'unconditional' 'engraft' contract of "Penumbra Doctrine." The "in personam" or possession of the 'person' who is being sued by a sow's ear contract in Admiralty, are now termed 'person of interest' by 'reasoned cause' and 'made liable,' because it is easy for agency to use the Dragon's elliptical words with 'public policy' blessing, because we 'volunteered.' When the citizen perjures the oath, it is 'made' a 'criminal' act by agency. There is no amount of lipstick that will cover that kiss.

Signature of the personam to agency is assent of a free Citizen 'person' and gives the court jurisdiction to do in personam action when silk purse 'dishonors' a 'promise' under penalty of perjury. 'In personam' jurisdiction cannot be had when Rights are reserved and Federal Rule 12. (b) may supply Remedy. We should never perjure our flag, but the Federal flag has its place and the republic flag has my silk purse.

An immigrant becomes a Citizen of the United States by signature to an 'unconditional' document. The 'person' is sworn to oath and allegiance and becomes in personam or possessed by his new 'master,' Article I Legislative and 'forum' Admiralty of Article II. This has become the executive master to us all, because both the wolf and Thee Sheep covet sow's ears. We Thee People are Alpha with Truth of Law and the stranger must absorb the nips. Citizen status varies in that a state Citizen has 'entitlement' to Thee Bill of Rights. The stranger or U.S. Citizen has no such Right.

Police power of Article II Executive/Admiralty is a 'rebutable presumption' to state Citizen for anything less than "crime." The immigrant left his natural personam in his native Land and contracted in personam, as 'strangers' are required, and became "a Citizen of the United States" at Art. II, Sec. 1, Cl. 5. If you moved to France, you would be an in personam subject citizen. The immigrant is now an 'artificial' citizen and 'person' of the 14th Amendment and 'subject' of this "New Covenant" Nation. Their rights are 'fair and impartial' due process of statute Article I and other "civil" Liberties.

Corporations and municipalities take similar oath and sign 'unconditional' documents and are 'artificial persons' by contract. Agency 'persons' birthright is Legislated Statute staple to the 14th Amendment due process and civil right Liberties. 'Subject' Citizens consent to Legislation and become "persons" of subject matter only jurisdiction and agree to be policed by "public policy," this is not the yoke of a Freeman.

The 'unconditional' signing gives agency executor 'power of attorney' to 'act in your stead' when issue arises at administrative 'dishonor or execution' of contract. If the issue is 'dishonored' by the contracted Citizen and cannot be resolved, an Article I agency Tribunal will hear the 'subject matter' dispute, IF Magistrate has the TWO jurisdictions required for 'competent' Tribunal. The most important ONE is in personam, which represents to the world that another silk purse Sovereign has fallen to the wolf.

Black's Law 5th. Subject matter. Nature of cause of action, and of relief sought.

The 2nd required jurisdiction is subject matter, which depends upon the 'subject' status in personam for suit of negotiable contract, and its material of situs. Agency 'must' follow the 'charter' of its maker in exercising its 'implied' and 'inferior' police power for it is limited to 'subjects' by signature to their sow's ear contract. If the proper 'subject' Citizen is on the Administrative record with assent to Maritime contract, there will be no need for a 'crime' to have been committed or 'probable cause' for indictment and warrant, the sow's ear will do just

5

fine with 'subject matter' 'information' of 'public policy' only. 'Without' personam, We Thee People Stand next to the soldier, salute smartly and take our leave, only with permission.

State Sovereign Citizens are "entitled" at Art. IV, Sec., 2, Cl. 1 to demand Article III Judiciary if the 'answer' to agency 'presentment' is 'timely, on point,' 'without dishonor,' or other "affirmative defense." The Separation of Powers protects the silk purse at "reservation" of Rights as "the privilege of the writ of habeas corpus shall not be suspended," Art. I, Sec. 9, Cl. 2. The Power of the Supreme Court will Stand for Thee state Citizen who 'Represents' himself with 'clean hands.' Of late the Supreme Court of the Land has not heard such a "prayer," for Law questions have been decided with "tacit" assent in signature to 'made actions' in personam, which have us yoked and "made liable" to 'unconscionable' sow's ears and UCC 2-302 is Remedy.

The jury, by 'procedure,' only needs to hear 'facts' and the judge "instructs" the 'law' the 'subject' defendant committed against public insurance policy and corporations. "Social engineering" has done its educational system very proud. The wiggly tail must not blind the silk purse to 'unconscionable' submission to the sow's ear or fraud is upon any instrument of Penumbra. A moth to this flame is just as "dead in law."

It does not matter at this point which birthright is before the Tribunal, all US silk purse Citizens and strangers sign the same sow's ear contracts. Agency mischief is 'without' our personam if we contract with 'condition.' Having a license to do or not to do a 'thing' has 'made liable' Sovereign personam to in personam 'action.' If you put a 'condition' such as "Without Prejudice" UCC 1-207 above your signature on the license, W-4, 1040, ferret bill of sale or bank account you 'reserve Rights' to your personam and the Tribunal is "without in personam jurisdiction" per Rule 12 (b), the issue is abated, and is as "dead in law" as the moth. You are non-assumpsit and did not 'promise' to appear, for a "condition" must not be written upon the instrument, Thee condition makes a unit non-negotiable.

Nature of subject matter is Article I statute and for 'facts,' there is no better place. The IRS alone will smother a citizen with facts. Civil law uses devise, presumption, voidable contract, and statute police powers if Rights are not reserved. An 'action' cannot be brought against a knowledgeable 'Personam' 'within' Thee Bill of Rights unless 'criminal intent' is probable in cause.

When a state Citizen becomes a soldier he/she gives up the Bill of Rights by signature to an 'unconditional' contract, which is not "unconscionable." The document gives agency 'in personam' personal 'promise' to be 'made liable' as the W-4 negotiable instrument also presumes. You may rebut the presumption of the W-4 by reserving your "entitled" Rights to exemption. The sow's ear instrument may be 'sued out' to compel performance of obligation, and you are now a sworn 'thing in action' as a 'subject' U.S. Citizen. The crime committed is 'dishonor' or failure to pay under penalty of perjury to follow oath and 'promise.' Municipal police power is the same incorporated 'public policy' oath of jus civis. The State cannot be a victim, unless by contract. When your personam forces agency to prove police power exist, in "fact of the matter stated," they will go away. Be meek, protect your personam silk purse at all times and keep thy words Truth.

We Thee People further reserve our Rights at Article IV Section 2 Clause 1; The Citizens of each state shall be entitled to all Privileges and Immunities of Citizens in the several states.

In order to have "entitlement" the state Citizen must "pray" for Thee Bill of Rights, not at all a bad idea. I had to wipe off a lot of lipstick to accomplish this task and with 'clean hands' I now sojourn freely. The wolf has seldom seen witness and dares not depart from nips at the sheep least We Thee People scatter.

Black's Law 5th. Entitle. In its usual sense, to entitle is to give a right or legal title to. (cite omitted)

To 'give' a right would be Legislative Civil Statute of 14th Amendment. A 'reservation' of rights 'represents' personam and 'legal title to' Article III Judiciary, a U.S. Citizens does not. The sow's ear was just a curly tail before the 14th Amendment. Supreme Court and its "decision" play the curly tail over Thee Silk Person of Dred Scott. This decision dealt a 'presumptive' blow to state Citizenship, which has forever suffered the 'Penumbra' glare of its 'devise' at Law.

The silk purse must commit a 'crime' 'intentionally' and have an actual silk purse "victim" and Thee People must "indict" the errant brother, prior to incarceration if the issue were "criminal." The sow's ear agency of State cannot be a victim and use police power to summon the silk purse 'without right.' Agency use of presumptive 'delict' and police powers is the blood of the sow's ear, and yet NO foundation. Truth cannot be "made," and the false teachers are found.

The 'Privileges and Immunities' of a state Citizen's silk purse is enumerated in the Bill of rights. Our 'entitlement' is "Rights to benefits, income or property which may not be abridged without due process" of Thee Bill of Rights, not through agency or IRS type 'inferior' Tribunal. U.S. subject Citizen due process is of the 14th Amendment 'fair and impartial.' "Indictment" of Thee People at Grand Jury is another place a sow's ear is not welcome unless the flag of Admiralty 'lies' upon it in its corporate 'nature.'

A state Citizen, is born a silk purse in a corporate State hospital, receives a birth certificate 'devise' of corporate nature, which is 'unconditionally' signed by the parents, and 'baptizes' the Sovereign born child into a nation of 'subjects' by negotiating the 'unconditional' sow's ear 'devise.' The social security 'devise' acts to cloud Rights of state born Sovereign to 'subject' U.S. Citizenship status, which has made the whole Gentile family of man 'domestic product.' Instead of just a few 'subjects,' the sow's ear will allow all the silk purses to sign as 'persons' via the 14th Amendment and 'claim' them all as Citizens of Penumbra beast doctrine.

'Personam' 'MUST' be guarded with knowledge of Truth or waived to the "Penumbra" beast in ignorance. I have thought hard about taking that 'old

Dragon Lobe, but not yet. I have settled with the beast that lobe is yours and Our Father forbids we bring corruption of blood to her.

The Sovereign of Man awaits obedience of Law. The Shepherd must depend upon Law for His lost Sheep. The flock is precious and the good Shepherd must take authority with a little salt to find the words to heal an issue of Law. Many of the lost have simply too much worry for the Shepherd and seek counsel elsewhere. Teaching is as easy as taking ignorance to "want" of knowledge. Truth is the only proper derivative of Law, and must always be at quest, least the Sovereign Church loose sight of the old Dragon.

A soldier's choice to give up his personam to the Executive Branch and become 'Government Issue' is a voluntary act. Soldier in personam and Article III are no longer married, for his waived Bill of Rights is now diverse with U.S. Citizenship by Article II Maritime Contract Law.

The soldier has a silk purse contract because his 'in personam' knows what a soldier's duty is. After the discharged soldier signs civilian 'unconditional' instruments 'without' his state Citizenship, he gets the sow's ear cluster, Penumbra. He has waived state Citizenship for U.S. Citizenship without knowing what he has done. A passport would contain the 'silk purse' name, as a U.S. Citizen, a W-4, application for employment or license would not, because you waive state Citizenship upon assent to the sow's ear if you do not reserve Rights.

The 'writing' at UCC 3-104.1 'must' be 'unconditional' at 3.104.2 to sustain a 'promise' at 3-104.3. Prima facie 'Condition' provides Remedy. Agency fails to disclose the waived status of your 'personam' state Citizenship. The 'negotiable instrument Law' is 'Registered' Federal Agency Law and it is also state Citizen friendly, because 'liability' is limited to 'subjects' only per "immunities and entitlement," which is why it is Law of Thee People.

Black's Law 5th. Negotiable document of title. A document is negotiable if by its terms the goods are to be delivered to "bearer," or to the order of a named party, or, where recognized in overseas trade, to a named person "or assigns." UCC 7-104.1.

The instrument is negotiable only when it is signed 'unconditionally' and under the penalty of perjury. The contract banner flag of Admiralty waves as a 1st class silk purse gold fringe in a parade, but a sow's ear when hung in state courtrooms and our children's schools, for it is recognition of Maritime Oath to Executive Branch of Article II. The enrollment assents to the banner 'devise,' ingratiating Thee Flag of the 'several states' in our libraries. All recognize this banner to represent the Maritime Commerce flag; it is not only beautiful, the banner is very serious in its intent and meaning. All state Citizens who sign aboard, represent themselves as 'subject' citizens of 'public policy' and due only sow's ear "subject matter" only justice of Admiralty. The good news is; there must be a viable Maritime contract dealing with Admiralty issues. Neither a politician of Article I nor General of Article II will admit to this jurisdiction for it is 'clothed' with elliptical 'engraft' 'color of Law.' Thee silk purse must feed Thee Truth to agency with a stick. I used Thee Staff of Moses and that big old Dragon just smiled, because I think she recognized IT.

Black's Law 5th. Uniform Code. Many states have adopted the Uniform Code of Justice, and others have adopted acts substantially following the Uniform Code.

The small 's' in state means your silk purse has 'forum' pig's ear on it. The Admiralty flag is very obtuse and because the Tribunal is using its 'devise' to its comfort, it must have your unconditional signing or jurisdiction cannot be 'made' at Rule 12 (b). 'Substantially following' the Admiralty Code, has led to state Citizens being assigned as 'person of interest' in gang sweeps and medicine being withheld without proper 'indictment.' Only the Beast has moaned for victim cannot be found least we forget the sick and our ferret friends.

Schoolyards are a natural ground for silk purses to gather in knowledge. Enrollment to the sow's ear allows sister Penumbra to use its implied police powers under 'devise' contract at the public school enrollment. The same silk purse from the "gang sweep" cannot be a 'thing in action' at his home or on the street without 'probable cause.' The school children are in a 'public policy' playground and easy to catch and are contracted 'birds of a feather.' What victim or 'crime' deserved the sow's ear?

No Rights were violated by the police power at the school for the 'subject' students have agreed per parental consent to agency in personam and to the possession of the child's silk purse person. "Public Law" of personam protects the children off school grounds where no nexus exist between Article I agency and Article III state Citizen. School jurisdiction cannot exist 'without' agency territorial borders. If only one of the silk purses would have reserved their Rights at enrollment it would have been a great day because that particular silk purse has no contract with agency and "crime" must have been committed before providing corporate sow's ear protection or 'public policy' police of the Penumbra Dragons.

All state citizens face the same type of situation. Our state public policy uses Federal Rules of police power as a means to civil authority. Jurisdiction of agency is confined to sow's ear subject matter and U.S. Citizens. Reasonable cause is merely a step up the chain of Admiralty when a state Citizen may be held as 'a person of interest.' All U.S. Citizens are under contract and oath. The Citizen then 'promises' he will follow the guidelines for subjects of Federal Citizenship, which were chosen upon admission into the 'forum' system per contract. You contracted for your own arrest and waived your Bill of Rights, you are now restricted to the forum you now find yourself.

Where is your mother? She taught her little silk purse the right thing to do and barely made error of it. Agency has difficulty with man because we wiggle. To agency Thee Bill of Rights is time consuming and a little more expensive but, if the proper elliptical Penumbra is used unconditionally, the unsuspecting pork is ready for market.

14th Amendment subjects are served well by attorneys and prosecutors, and police power of Federal Law. When following the procedures at Tribunal before an "inferior" judge of the Department of Justice, there is no need for a 'crime,' only mother 'public policy' need bring action and subject matter of a "made liable" in personam Citizen.

There are several ways to stray into Federal custody. "Devise" of elliptical contractual units signed unconditionally is the most prevalent. Understanding you have violated "public policy" may be tacit, but gives jurisdiction. Lawyer who 'stand in your stead' have filed 'answers' to the Tribunal. In Personam and on record as obedient to the Rules of Procedure will carry the day after the judge allows the jury to hear facts only. No Law will be heard because the silk purse has waived all issues per lawyer or in tacit.

I, on the silk purse state Citizenship side of this pasture, pray to God every day for His Mercy and understanding. Knowledge of my Covenant Citizenship is the same Law that resides within the Bill of Rights and Article III Judiciary. St. Mathew 6:32.

State Citizens enjoy a much better managed system of "entitled" "privileges and Immunities" of Law at Article 4 Section 2 Clause I. Being entitled does not make the Bill of Rights automatic. We Thee People are required to have "clean hands" prior to issue or jurisdiction in personam is a reality and becomes fact of Law on the administrative record. We are bound to the 'subject matter' of the fact stated and the jurisdiction of Tribunal.

We Thee People must ask individually for our Rights. If an unconditional contract with agency exists, it must be voided ab initio, or agency will treat the contract as "satisfaction and accord" and proceed. The Administrative record will reflect the fact that your signature is valid and you have 'dishonored' the instrument at 'promise.' A good record for the judge would contain affidavits of revocation of signature, which takes away the police power to action. The appearance of "without prejudice" on any document at action will mean "woe ye lawyers" and judges, because a silk purse will have a pig's ear in a Title 18.

A state Citizen is "immune" to Federal procedures and "privileged" to use the Bill of Rights. The judge of Article III will hear no prejudice or 'devise.' A "crime" will have been committed against another silk purse or fraud of agency, but tried by Article III Judiciary. No police power exists until the state Citizen violates an enumerated "public Law," at "probable cause," statute notwithstanding.

Black's Law 5th. Assigns. Assignees; those to whom property is, will, or may be assigned. Used e.g. in the phrase, in deeds, "heirs, administrators, and assigns to denote the assignable nature of the interest or right created." It generally comprehends all of those who take either immediately or remotely from or under the assignor, whether by conveyance, devise, descent, or act of law. This serpent tongue is radiant with presumption of how we all fall to the brilliant darkness of the Penumbra sphere. The words 'assignable' and 'rights created' sounds so much like Maritime contract that, yes; I believe it is. Truth is, no rights are of Agency, without assent to its 'devise'. 'Created rights' of agency are of your own 'right hand,' with assent of 'forehead.'

God created you as a silk purse to do His work. Agency 'creation' of devise to contract the politics of the sow's ear is void of fairness. Without a representation of Rights on any document, which appears to be agency, would not be excellent counsel. The Citizen 'assigns the nature' of remote 'devise' to agency as 'in personam' and becomes actionable by assent and possession to police power. Acts of Law are anything the Citizen signs, which "made liable" his 'obligation of contract,' or confiscation of his ferret 'within' the Article II forum, even at parole, taxation, or garnishment. Maritime issues are for soldiers, not the silk purse state Citizen. Federal Law may only 'indict' a silk purse for Treason. The state Citizen is "immune" to Federal Prosecution per Article IV Section 2 Clause 1 of the Constitution. God is King of this Land, and "represents" Thee Sovereign Silk Purse. We Thee People may enjoy His Liberty via the Grace of "immunity and privilege" in Thee name of Jesus.

The Fish and Game Agency of California will confiscate a pet ferret in a heartbeat. The agency is powerless to 'take' 'property' of a state Citizen who has protected their interest 'Without Prejudice' UCC 1-207 upon the bill of sale. The use of the medicinal marijuana card serves notice upon any sow's ear agent that you are a silk purse when you reserve your Rights "Without Prejudice" UCC 1-207 above your personam signature on the card, contract or license. Immunity to the police power of the State begins with a "notice of "entitlement" via reservation of your Citizenship status Rights. The individual Citizen must protect their ferret, tax, and school children or loose them as 'contraband,' which is a fancy name for 'unrepresentative' or uninsured Citizen Property. Doctors and professionals who are licensed may reserve Rights on license and/or memorandums of understanding, whether state or Federal "forum." Burden of proof falls to the accuser and even ignorance can be protected by silence.

A responsible parent who would like to have their child in extra curricular activities without blood test or hear a speech on God must protect those Rights by reserving them. Otherwise it is presumed that the child is under the rules of Admiralty and the MPs will be back to your schoolyard to prevent 'public policy' Citizens from mischief and using the name of God in "other needful buildings" of Art. 1, Sec. 8, Cl. 17.

A 'devise,' which 'captures' the state Citizen to assent his 'personam' as 'prize' and not disclose, is 'piracy,' AFTER NOTICE. Maritime Law is of the "Penumbra Doctrine" engraft and void ab initio upon 'peremptory' 'rebuttal' as "affirmative defense" by the vigilant Citizen.

When knowledge of the old Dragon serpent is understood, Grace will covet your heart and guide your right hand to Remedy. God is Sovereign, and so are His silk purses. We Thee People must not render unto the sow's ear that which is not the old Dragon's anyway. She has the share of more than we, but Truth shall set what We Gentiles All Have, Free.

Thee Citizen has the Right to see copy of a valid instrument with verified signature of BOTH parties at issue by using UCC 3-505 'counter demand.' Agent 'capacity to act for another' is very limited in 'charter corporations'. Agent becomes personally liable for violating a state Citizen's Rights and is 'made liable' to the citizen under Title 18.

Black's Law 5th. Maritime Law. That which the Congress has enacted or in the Federal courts, sitting in admiralty, or in the exercise of their maritime jurisdiction, have declared and would apply. All statutes, acts and codes are law for territorial 'subject' Citizens. Article I Legislative 'declared'; statutes apply to 'subjects' and 'matter' of its maker, ONLY, unless the unwary Sovereign stumbles into the State 'forum' court, which displays the Admiralty flag in 'treaty' with the United States. Soldiers, immigrants, and 'corporate America'; all, every one have sworn to the 'benefit' of welfare and safety of Admiralty. Federal Court Rules of Procedure at 12 (b) mandate 'subject' citizens' 'must' be 'unconditionally' contracted within Admiralty 'devise' or tacitly 'made liable' for the Tribunal to have jurisdiction. It actually says the administrative record must show jurisdiction in personam and subject matter.

To make this pig wiggle, let's add a "condition of non-assumpsit" to this Jezebel and cut off the "promise" at the wiggly tail and BAM, sausage for Article II only, I am having beef at the table of Thee Supreme Law Court.

'Personam' issues are decided prior to trial; you gave agency an in personam waiver to your God Given Bill of Rights and took the Law of man to worry. You are a now a signed Citizen of Washington District and bound by statutes replete of state Law.

I just now noticed my use of 'may be ugly,' but not worrisome enough to change too. My personam Choice is; you do not care about the 'in Thee Work,' but "of its content." You see I view this writing a 'silk purse of pearls,' and jesters to the use of 'are hereby rebutted.' That's all I have to say about that!

A docket is the administrative record of action, and the 'exercise' of Admiralty's 'Penumbra Doctrine' department Head; Maritime jurisdiction. You're written permission to 'action' is upon the W-4, license, bank account, or school registration instrument in case you 'dishonor' 'public policy' statute. The burden is for Citizen to prove his innocence, as it should be because you did agree to 'terms' without right to your personal Covenant.

I found Law, to better any amount of facts you can possibly represent. If a silk purse does not go "within" the "unconditional" contract by non assumpsit, which is "without prejudice UCC 1-207," you stay "without" its negative terms of assumpsit, because the unit is "unconscionable" at UCC 2-302. If your choice was to sign 'unconditionally' as the soldier, you waived your heritage to statute 'devise.' The soldier knows the government is taking his personal Rights, Thee state Citizen does not, and waives the right of "innocent until proven guilty" of "crime." Failure to disclose, I think so!

"Without prejudice" as condition to your personam abates in personam actions and police powers attached thereto. Non-assumpsit means "I do not partake," and issue at bar "cannot be used as evidence against" you, it "will not sustain a promise" of bail or appearance, ferret license or helmets and "a man may have his peace, when he knows the signing is without Right," while being surrounded by MPs, ferrets, pirates and "held," in court or otherwise. The "promise" follows the unconditional signing at UCC 3-104.3. No harm, no foul. No pig's ear on your silk purse.

The maritime cite goes on to say "OR in the exercise of their maritime jurisdiction," which is the "subject matter" gold fringe ensnaring Thee Flag of We Thee People's silk purses. "That which Congress has enacted" is a very clear warning at display of the Admiralty flag. The same flag is teaching our schools that the Bible is not welcome in Thee Discovery of Knowledge. These are the places where Thee People gather for Truth of the 'pearls' within Thee silk purse, only to waive the Rights to Freedom of Choice prima facie on a sow's ear enrollment 'devise.' Admiralty is the police power unless the vigilant's ears are to the ground of Truth.

The heavy Staff of Moses is thrown to this Ground and Law of God has prevailed. We Thee People are of excellent character and know Thee Law. Romans 2:14.

Congress enacts 'statutes staple' to guide and track the U.S. Citizen 'residing' within your state per the 14th Amendment. If an ignorant Sovereign wants to join the fleet, o.k, attrition of the faithful is a maritime 'domestic' strategy of democratic 'public policy' against U.S. sheeple. Institutions must obligate Thee blind sheep of silk purses to concentrate on public policy issues. Unconditionally signing agency corporate instruments leaves no wiggle or room to do it in.

When signing a contract "unconditionally,' you become a 'thing' of 'action' 'in personam" and agency has captured your Personam flag. Thee Bill of Rights, was your soldier general at signature and you left it to serve another flag 'in want' of political skills at public Law. You waived your Bill of Rights 'unconditionally' under penalty of perjury oath. You have become a U.S. Citizen and 'subject' to its jurisdiction of Admiralty.

When a silk purse reserves rights, and confiscation occurs, it is 'piracy' and action may be taken to the centurion at Title 18. Jesus never turned His cheek to a violent blow and neither should you. It takes Knowledge of the beast to be "as wise." The "dove of peace" is from your "forehead" to your heart and Truth will overtake the sow's ear with just a little help from Thee "Right Hand," which Scribe Thee rights.

Article I Section 8 Clause 17. To exercise exclusive Legislation in all cases whatsoever, over such District (NOT exceeding ten Miles square) as may, by Cession of particular States, and the acceptance of congress, become the Seat of the Government of the United States, and to exercise like Authority over all places purchased by the consent of the Legislature of the State in which the Same shall be, for the Erection of forts, Magazines, Arsenals, dockyards, and other needful Buildings:

By 'devise' only do We Thee People suffer this Citizenship Diversity! A District instrument 'executed' within a state is Piracy, unless the 'thing in action' and silk purse assents to valid Maritime contract. People know little about the Penumbra "Sphere." The light of it is as beautiful as an Admiralty flag in a schoolyard, and just as harmful to us silk purses. When the silk purse is blinded, it forces the head down, which makes Thee "Stand" difficult, and master has controls least we wiggle.

All this mayhem is confined within the 1-8-17 District. Spillover into your silk purse state is ignorance at acceptance of the unconditional contract of Maritime jurisdiction. The Citizen is left with license to a wiggly tail and BAM, "forum color of law" due process with police power. Congress voted, or you 'unconditionally' signed something that makes all Citizenship status quid pro quo for 'domestic product' obligation purposes. The good news; applies to "subjects" ONLY.

The Military code of justice put the sow's ear into your silk purse state public 'District' schoolyard by assent. 'Subjects' violated 'public policy' that is forbidden to its contracted Citizens. The law of the Beast will put more sow's ear contract before the silk purse, and they will sign as "memorandum of understanding" its contents and addendum to the administrative record of the Child's enrollment or court docket. If the silk purse does not obligate to the instrument, he has 'dishonored' the "promise," on his enrollment, enlistment or W-4 and executor awaits the straggler with presentment and police power.

Shortly after an Article I act, statute or 'devise' of Congress has been passed, it goes to the President. In order to allow the 'execution' of the Territorial District law of Maritime jurisdiction; the President at Article II must sign the instrument 'unconditionally' to execute its 'forum' to the States or Territories of sow's ear 'devise,' OR send it back. With a wave and pens trophied, the Executor creates life unto the District of corporate American 'subjects.' I do not live in their land and they have no Sovereign Rights over me. I am part Irish, but I do not tribute Ireland for my American state Citizenship. I am also part American Indian, but no birth certificates were available at the time and I cannot "prove" my "claim." Our forefathers knew these issues in their heart and Golden Law of We Thee People has sojourned to this pass; to go uncensored, unchallenged, or at least seemingly unnoticed as the sheep among the wolf.

Police powers of reasonable "action" extend only 'within' the Territorial District, "probable cause" will stand Thee Wall within your state border as personam. 'Persons' 'subject to the jurisdiction thereof' the sow's ear covenant are 'made liable' by 'enrollment.' The MP jurisdiction and police power ends once he is off his "subject matter," 'reservation,' or Territory. Wherever a state Citizen is found in want of public policy, he is "immune" thereto and enjoys the "privilege" of "public Law."

Thee state has Article III police power reserved to Thee People at the X Amendment and Military Courts cannot extend to the Supreme Court 'in action' against a state Citizen who has reserved his personam unless treason is probable.

Dred Scott suffered this "yoke" of 'devise' because his personam birthright was wrongfully 'executed' in personam by statute in the Supreme Court. Pursuit by the MPs must end at the state border or the State 'forum' is partner in benefit of the Mercantile Contract. W-4 and schoolyard are the best examples, and God loves his ferrets.

The problem with MPs, you must give notice of your state Citizenship "entitlement" status and 'immunity' or agency will treat you like you have a sow's ear agreement, and it is then open season on silk purses.

Notice to agency is Truth of your natural Law entitlement. MP action by sow's ear of that Truth is actionable by the silk purse against the sow's ear 'implied' police power agent personally. The sow's ear at instrumenvt must be put on 'notice' that the greed and power of its master must ONLY 'imply' 'inferior' law and even that is rebutted.

When we counsel our brother with Thee Shepherds knowledge and Authority, we must know that Thee Truth was Covenant. The Church is forfeit if the false teacher is not a sign of warning. Government is doing the same for us, the best it can, and no one should take a stick to its agents.

You might stamp your Shepherds Staff in support of Thee Staff of Moses and pray, for We Thee People are in Posterity. God awaits Authority of Law and Truth for Church, for thereby Thee Lost are Found.

All agency needs to hear in 'answer' to presentment is that you are a silk purse personam and you made an "unconscionable" and voidable contract, "without dishonor." Only then will they go away until YOU need something. Do not hide from the red light in the mirror; the Beast does not leave pray on the run, for once caught in 'devise' the plague of false teaching will engulf the many heads of Penumbra by its own 'conveyance.'

Proper words will remedy the issue and preserve your Rights. Implied police power requires an 'enabling clause' to use its delict on the silk purse. Police powers may subject only their own sow's ear contracts and not invade the privities, which are silk purse state Citizen at Article III.

Black's Law 5th. Enabling clause. That portion of a statute or constitution, which gives the government officials the right to put into effect and to enforce such.

Statutes are for 'subjects,' whether by state 'devise' or Federal 'forum'. One power may not 'engraft' or interfere with the others purses and ears contracts. The enabling power of an 'unconditional' signing brings the sow's ear MP to your "other needful building" schoolyard, because your in personam 'enabled' the police power with 'implied' 'action' and in fact 'with right' per contract. IF you happened to be a silk purse, caught in the 'sweep,' all Rights are reserved in your New Sovereign Covenant with God of Law. No searches, seizures, arrest, or confiscated ferrets. Crime against your neighbor would not show Love, for thereby we 'dishonor' Thee Law Master. God is to be Loved, not tempted with judgment. All are anointed who follow Thee Golden Rule.

Black's Law 5th. Enabling statute. Term applied to any statute enabling persons or corporations to do what before they could not. It is applied to statutes, which confer new powers.

'Persons' or corporations are a created class of artificial citizens Of 14th Amendment and void of personam Rights. Police powers are enacted and enabled for these subject citizens only, via Executive/Admiralty. Remember, all statutes of Congress, are Admiralty by design and mandatory dictate for subject citizens ONLY.

The state Citizen can shout "immunity" from the mountaintops because the enabler is forbidden to touch one Right of the silk purse unless a 'crime' is committed. If the MPs set foot on your sacred ground, they are effectively put on notice of your "natural Law" Choice to reserve Rights and to have Thee People 'indict' rather than be flesh of the sow's ear. The sow's ear is 'in want' of Thee Silk Purse, just say NO! There is no amount of 'devise' or lipsticks that will allow 'implied power' of greed or wiggly tail to intercede with my Silk Purse.

Your political signature has 'made liable' your personam to any instrument you sign 'unconditionally,' for in personam jurisdictional purposes of agency and action. 'Public policy' is Congressional mandate of 'social engineering' and We Thee People have waived knowledge of Law heritage. UCC 3-104.2 'unconditional' is the key to reserving personam. An instrument signed with a CONDITION looses your Generalship to do 'action' at Article III and the Bill of Rights at Amendment V, instead of sow's ear due process at 14th Amendment.

'Without Prejudice' UCC 1-207, signed above your signature, 'represents' the Bill of Rights and your "Immune" Personam Sovereign heritage, which is attached thereto as 'notice' to agency at UCC 1-102.26. Your personam is now with you and free from agency 'issues' because the signing was 'conditional,' non-assumpsit and no 'promise' may 'sustain' an 'appearance' that is gotten by 'devise,' or while agency bears weapons of 'domestic war.' Therefore, no contract exists because you reserved your personam right to 'confess and avoid' fraud of 'bearer' and the instrument is 'non-negotiable,' because you are not an 'in personam/thing in action,' nor kin' of the sow's ear. Habeas Corpus; a "freeman' is being 'held" by 'devise' 'in want' of jurisdiction. The trier of fact will have none of this wiggly tail issue, or he be smitten with Jezebel and "made liable" to the personam Citizen at Title 18 "color of Law" action and the judge will drag every agent who actioned you with him.

Black's Law 5th. Maritime Law. Substantially, in the United States, it is federal law, and jurisdiction to administer it is vested in the federal courts, though not to the entire exclusion of the courts of the states.

Federal courts are Article II and alien entirely to the Bill of Rights and Article III. How much more obvious is elliptical from Truth. Federal laws are for 'subject' 'persons' of federal citizenship. Federal flag equals 'inferior' State law of Admiralty and a valid Maritime contract must exist upon the Administrative record or the issue cannot be heard at Rule 12. (b). Your Rights cannot be violated in this court IF, you reserved your Right of non-assumpsit, or "I do not partake" of the jurisdictional in personam instrument.

Black's Law 5th. Federal Citizenship. Rights and obligations accruing by reason of being a citizen of the United States. State or status of being a citizen of the United States.

The God Created Rights of the state Citizen are enumerated in Thee Bill of Rights and et seq. Articles. U.S. Citizen's 'accrue' rights via statute at 'incola' or inhabitant 'resident' rather than 'domicile' civis Juris. Look it up! That flick at your 'cheek' is not the silk purse found 'within' Thee Bill of Rights, but the 'tongue' 'slap' of the old dragon beast tugging at your Pearls. 'State' means Territories of which there are at least seven and all 'residents' are 'subject' to its master via there own Admiralty flags and they may as well reside in the District. Thee states are protected by the stars and stripes, blues, whites and red, but only in time of emergency should there be a gold fringe in our schools and even then Thee Bill of Rights is not suspended.

The state courts can stand the shock of change, but our children cannot if We Thee People do not realize the plight of our "other needful building" schoolyard. Our children must receive "competent counsel" or take issue between each other and form protective groups to identify themselves as family. The children will mature and become the parent to raise their own 'domesticated' family for the sake of "public policy."

A state Citizen is Sovereign to all men of his peers, with Rights inalienable to his personam status as non-resident to the sow's ear and Domiciled at state Citizen. BUT, Thee Citizen must be vigilant for the 'purse' makes a lousy 'ear' and certainly no Pearls are found within.

Beware of the greatest duplicator of all creation, and his Penumbra Beast. Eyes, dark to see but for the faint yet bright light sphere of Thee Brilliant Star it shadows. A star is to come and fool those who would have belief in false teaching. To have his inferior 'glory' unto God, he must be an authoritive businessman and honor Obligations of Maritime Contract. A U.S. Citizen does not own anything that is not built on knowledge and the Truth of it. We Gentiles who have ears are listening but need put more Law Staff to ground. Authority of Thee Shepherd must fruit Thee Seed of Thee Lost to Glorify Thee return of Jesus with Law and Truth of Thee Church.

Article I courts are 'inferior' to Article III because its jurisdiction may try 'subject matter' only. Subject matter is the contract you signed and the issues that arise from it concerning such 'things' as presumptive reasonable cause, 'person of interest,' 'information,' and obligation of the contracted amount you are 'made liable' to remit.

Article II police power may obligate its citizens and Territories any way they will, as long as they do not condemn an innocent. Not one of the democratic, corporate characters of 'public policy' cares, unless the 'thing' is not insured. If not insured then any old deep silk purse will do and agency may by 'devise' adulterate law in 'color' for police power to obtain any unrepresentative 'thing in action' they wish.

When Thee People are victim of 'crime' and hold our errant brother in prison, it is to be the 'peers' best understanding of "Public Law." God reserves rights to those lost and his Law is not locked out. Those who did not commit "crime" with 'intent' are the innocents who are judged "fair and impartially" by their "public policy" fellow and "condemned" 'without right,' for the sake of the State.

17

The Citizen who prays to Article III Judiciary and republican 'Public Law' inherit the Bill of Rights, which "entitles" state Citizenship "privileges and immunities." None of the three powers may infringe upon the Obligation of Contract that each enjoy. Article III is bared by your contract with Article II and cannot come to your defense, you must pray it as a 'personam state Citizen' at situs 'without' the chartered jurisdiction of agency. Then Thee Judiciary will hear your 'prayer' at UCC 1.103.6 where the "Common Law" is enforced. California Code 22.2 would also make good study, for the issue is then 'executed' by Thee Supreme Power of the Land, God's Common Law.

ONLY the Sovereign Citizen who maintains his personam may pray out of the Article I Tribunal, via the poor man's Habeas Corpus; "WITHOUT PREJUDICE" UCC I-207. The 'subject' U.S. Citizen would not have Grace at UCC 1.103.6. The Agency would however be severely restricted at the administrative charter and record. 'Mail box policy' presentments are agency weapons and must be answered with language of agency law or it will not 'ear' your words. Facts are difficult to argue, so stick with Law. 'Parol' evidence and facts change with Legislation and agency elliptical "words of art," Law does not change.

All 'persons' 'made liable' by signing 'unconditional' instruments are 'subjects' of 'domestic product,' and by 'devise' U.S. Citizens. Little is known of the 'meek' of Thee 'republican' 'sheep' of New Covenant Law, for We Thee People have waived our Rights thereto.

The Gentiles have done well with Thee Law Staff of Moses. Thee Shepherd must teach his flock with Thee Authority written, for We Thee People must Stand this Rock and Pasture with the wolf. Faith in Thee Truth of Jesus and Knowledgeable Counsel with our Father gave Grace of Law to the Meek. God is once again Law Sovereign of a Nation, We Thee Gentile People of Thee united States of America are heirs.

The Ten Commandments are all 'represented' 'personam' within Thee Bill of Rights, which are the first Ten Amendments and the silk purse of the Constitution. Students beware of et. seq. Amendments, for no Sovereign Rights are found therein and thereby no law to subjugate, save the sow's ear, wiggly tail, or ferret.

Jurisdiction of the court to proceed with any claim relies on the 'justiciable' issues of fact and Law on the administrative record. Not everything we sign are of "satisfaction and accord" and when a reservation of rights is upon the instrument, it's challenged as 'dead in Law.' Agency must answer or assent your 'conditional' reservation of Rights or estoppel.

Jesus knew the proclivity of His adversary was not to answer, and that is exactly the response with which you may have Grace. Contracts of 'devise' are fraudulent for the Truth has not been told and are utterly void or estoppel. You must make those contracts 'dead in Law' by always reserving your personam, and thereby never waiving Rights for in personam action. Let the court figure it out; believe me the old Dragon will make it known that your silk purse is not 'actionable' or welcome for he protects the ears of others to the Truth.

A 'person' becomes a soldier or agency 'subject' by signature and oath of allegiance to obey statute and actions. The only remedy of 'actions' is Article II Executive estoppel at the Administrative Record of corporate State 'forum.' Agency 'without jurisdiction' of remedy sought, has no 'police power' ab initio. Where police power ends, Habeas Corpus at Article 1 Section 9 Clause 2 begins, if agency proceeds.

We Thee People are individually entitled to Thee Choice of Law. If you knew the Truth as I know it, there would be 'jubilees.' We Thee People 'reserve' the power to have the Federal Government protect the state, 'without its jurisdiction' over the Silk purses domiciled 'within' state borders and schoolyards.

    From:
    Domicile:
    City state:
    Certified post # Administrative Record/doc. # dated:

PROPRIA PERSONA Special Appearance de bene esse, non grant executory in personam and Abatement per Rule 12 (b)

    RE: Personam express representation estoppel to Agency Summons/Presentment, ACTS 22:25

    Attention agent: Notice: UCC 1-201.26, "Color of Law" 42 U.S.C.A.1983

I am appearing in Special Propria Personam and not General in personam to challenge presumption of Statute Procedural "due process" "action" of Tribunal in situs of Maritime jurisdiction. My writing of "Without Prejudice" is "Material Alteration and Evidence" at UCC 3-407.1. I "declare" my representation as notice of "entitlement to all Privileges and Immunities of the several states" at Article I Section 2 Clause I of the Constitution of the united States. Article III Judiciary and the Supreme Court has original jurisdiction of this case.

Agency police power is bound to Article I Statute at Negotiable Instruments Law of UCC 3-104.2. Activation of police power is "unconditionally" assented by "dishonor" of statute for "reasonable cause" and agency may "action' 'persons' of 'territorial subject matter jurisdiction" only at Article II.

I hereby refute, abrogate and void signature ab initio of agency presumptuous or "unconscionable" instruments at UCC 2-302 and any and all powers of attorney, "Without Dishonor." There are no de jure, certified, creditable, or negotiable instruments within the administrative record which obligate or assent waiver of state Citizen "Privilege" and exemption to de facto agency action. The UCC 3-104.1 instrument I "signed" was "conditional," for duress and "color of law" were at elliptical fraud upon the obligatory presentment. The "doctrine of estoppel by 'concealment and suppression' applies when there has been reduction to practice of invention" or devise. I am not "made liable" to appear or "promise" at UCC 3-104.3 and perjury is vitiated.

William Dixon

I am not knowledgeable in the law and I am without competent counsel. I deny Miranda attorney for it cannot represent Propria Persona and is admission to the jurisdiction of Territorial Statutory Maritime jurisdiction, tacit not withstanding.

Speaking Demurrer declares Rule 12 (b) dismissal and Amendment IV "probable cause, supported by oath or affirmation" for warrant of my Personam to be "certified" upon the administrative record.

There is no creditable witness "without color" and no victim of the common law certified on the record. California Code 22.2 requires the "statute be read in harmony with the common Law" as does the Article III Power within UCC 103.6.

I further "confess and avoid' 'out of court' 'to any person, official or otherwise' that there is a 'reasonable inference to the contrary," that probable cause is express and substantial upon the Administrative Record.

Administrative agent has 30 days to rebut and estoppel of agency is in effect. Please be specific in your "lawful" cause of action and include only substantive claim of agent.

Chapter 2: Penumbra Doctrine

I am, William, this witness to GOD AND HIS SOVEREIGN COVENANT of Law is my Blessing for the knowledge and GRACE of it. "Penumbra," is of implied power and adhesions of police power by Penumbra "engraft." We Thee People assent, and are individually 'made liable' by elliptical 'words of art' and agency activity.

ACTS: 28-28 "Be it known therefore unto you, that the salvation of God is sent unto the Gentiles, and that they will listen." This book is for those who hear the Penumbra sphere of light that blinds the heart.

The Constitution of these United States of America and a republic of Sovereign states under THE LAW OF GOD with JESUS CHRIST as intercede and "WITHOUT PREJUDICE" Uniform Commercial Code section 1-207.

Subject matter: Non-Fiction; Law of Thee Gentiles and "Truth of the matter stated."

Article I: Legislative Implied Power's, delegated police power, and Inferior courts are subject to the Uniform Commercial Code as dominate statute. Negotiable Instruments Law is subject to its master, Congress. A reservation of Rights is "declaration" of "entitlement" to personam Bill of Rights.

Article II: The Executive Power, Maritime jurisdiction, 14th Amendment, "Penumbra" police power at "reasonable cause," and "dishonor' of 'agency activity" obligation and UCC Remedy.

Article III: The Judicial Power, Supreme Court, Thee Bill of Rights, Separation of POWER Doctrine, Uniform Commercial Code 1-103.6, police power at "probable cause" and Penumbra.

God Bless those who hear the "cited."

Black's Law 5th. Penumbra doctrine. The implied powers of the federal government predicated (something assigned to a class; citizenship) on the Necessary and Proper Clause of the U.S. Const., Art. I, Sec. 8(18), permit one implied power to be engrafted on another implied power. Kohl v. U.S., 91 U.S. 367, 23 L.Ed. 449.

A Beast of diverse weights hath a name; Penumbra is factual devise of elliptical statutory procedures which engraft U.S. Citizens to Article I Legislative and Article II Maritime jurisdiction. Article I IRS is engraft of this beast and its life blood "must' unconditionally" negotiate "Obligation of Contract" and commercial intercourse among it's "made liable" subjects. Article I is "engraft" to Article II at police powers for taxing and "actions" upon a unit "dishonored' by 'subjects." Subject Citizen "persons" are required per agreement and oath to obligate and honor "unconditionally," all required license and Statutory Procedures. "Dishonored" units and taxes are collected per voluntary terms of agreement when Maritime jurisdiction is activated.

Fourteenth Amendment "due process" is designed to actuate police power with "reasonable cause" when these "persons" of U.S. Citizenship commit a wrong against another Citizen, licensed activity or agency obligation. "Persons" of the 14th Amendment are "municipal as are other government units within meaning of 42 U.S.C.A. 1983."

"A resident alien is a "person" within the meaning of the due process and equal protection clauses of the 14th Amendment." C.D.R. Enterprises, Ltd. v. Board of Ed. of City of New York, D.C.N.Y., 412 F. Supp. 1164, 1168.

A resident alien becomes a U.S. Citizen by "test," oath of loyalty and voluntary subjugation to Statutory Procedures of the United States Congress per Article 1 Section 8 Clause 17 and engraft of contractual Maritime Admiralty. Engraft of "persons" to obligation instruments does not violate Rights because of the "persons" voluntary assent, which is the goal of "public policy" and domestic product. A "Persons" only Rights are Civil in created nature and Maritime jurisdiction must be certifiable for Rule 12(b) to stand.

Article III Judicial is prohibited per the Separation of Powers to interfere with either Article I or Article II issues of voluntary contracts without a declaration of entitlement to Thee Bill of Rights. Artificial "persons" are not "entitled" to Bill of Rights and "pray" to the jurisdiction of Article III Supreme Court at Commerce Clause and 14th Amendment.

The State of California is a "person" when action is "made" against a subject Citizen for "dishonored" obligation or promise. Engraft assents police power with permission of the "resident" U.S. Citizen.

"Natural born Citizens" of the separate states are not U.S. Citizens and are not "Obligated to Contract" with any "person" without knowingly, willingly, and intentionally agreeing to terms. Penumbra has had her days with We Thee People and her engrafts are "unconscionable" and may be rejected.

Congressional "implied power" ENFORCEMENT of adhesions to 13th, 14th, 15th, 19th, 23rd, 24th, and 26th Amendments to the Sovereign Citizen are hereby challenged. Article 16th; has NO ENFORCEMENT Powers'. IRS uses "engraft" of Title 17 A.T.F. as "implied power" and Maritime jurisdiction. All "IMPLIED POWERS" are "vested" by the Negotiable Instrument Law and

Enforced by the Uniform Commercial Code at 3-104 (1) Signing, and (2) Unconditional, and (3) Promise.

Article-I "All legislative Power's' herein granted shall be vested in a congress of the United States." Courts have "made liable' their own corporate 'subjects' of 'government activity' and are controlled by the regulated 'Negotiable Instruments Law" and applicable police power attached thereto. "Implied Powers' are 'vested' ONLY within the "restricted" area of Article I Section 8 Clause 17. The 14th Amendment is "appropriate legislation of this article." The "vested' rights and powers are 'those enumerated' in 1-8-17, 'and all other powers vested by this Constitution in the government of the United States, or in any Department or Officer thereof." "Restricted" to Article I power ONLY. Those "subject' to Article I are 'made liable' to the 'inferior' courts of the democratic, artificial, public policy, municipality and commercial 'domestic product' 'persons," of the 14th Amendment. Their rights are secured by their faithful oath and application to have the status of a subject "person." Article I created the status, and the Article II Inferior court of Admiralty furnish obligation and tax license forum. This is a Law court which "must' have a 'power' by 'nexus' 'words of art' and devise contract to aggregate the masses of its subject 'persons." A contract with banks, motor vehicles, schools, employment, and even churches have "adhesions' for unknowing citizens that bind them to other 'Penumbra activity." Agency "implications of ownership by possession" are school children, W-4, vehicle registration, mortgages, Federal Reserve Accounting Unit Devise or FRAUDS. License type contracts for U.S. Citizens or the unwary state Citizen are waiting at the line. Our seduction has been meticulous, and We Thee People are "made liable' and 'subjected' to the 'vested" interest of Congress voluntarily.

The Sovereignty of state citizenship, under the Bill of Rights and Article III, shields the "natural born Citizen" from federal mischief of negotiable contracts and police power. We have the Right to contract, OR not, and we may scribe our own personal representation to ANY document that reads unconscionable.

'Negotiable Instrument' law defines the duties of Article I 'government activity' 'units." When contracting Penumbra with its corporate citizens, "presentment' 'must' be "unconditional" or the instrument is 'dead in law," NON-negotiable if the knowledgeable citizen has written a CONDITION, on the summons, license, or tax form, etc. The ferret hunting Fish and Game "persons' will not be able to use the instrument bearing your signature or statement to mischief and are 'made liable" individually if they violate their oath to the Constitution of These united States of America.

The Uniform Commercial Code is of Article I "making;" "an instrument 'must' meet the requirements set out in Section 3-104: it 'must' be in a writing signed by the 'maker' or 'drawer' (to cause to exist a bill or draft); it 'must' contain an (2) UNCONDITIONAL" (signature); (3) Promise...

A "government agency' gives notice to its citizens through 'facts' of its 'unconditional' rules and regulation, which are signed by the regulated citizen as 'drawer." These citizens are only "then' bound by 'agency activity' of Article I and 'subject' to its inferior courts of

'Civil 'commercial' venture" at Executive Maritime contract. The W-4 instrument "must' not be a "CONDITIONAL" contract by mutual negotiated agreement, for a requirement of negotiability is that the unit be "unconditional." Agency "words of art' seduce the unknowing to contracts, license, and the 'welfare and institutions' of our own 'making." Personam is waived to agency codes of procedure and police power as enforcer of Admiralty Maritime agreements. If you have made an "unconscionable" agreement or none at all, you are "entitled" to the Bill of Rights, and police power begins upon "indictment" of Thee People at "probable cause."

Black's Law 5th Separation of powers. The government of states and the United States are divided into three departments or branches: the legislative, which is empowered to make laws, the executive which is required to carry out the laws, and the judicial which is charged with interpreting the laws and adjudicating disputes under the laws. One branch is not permitted to encroach on the domain of another.

The states and the Federal government each have their own Constitutional Article covenant, and at least an effort is required to keep their powers separate from the other Articles. Legislative Congress passes Statute laws to control the subject citizens under their jurisdiction. These are foreign persons who obtain permission to reside or visit America and corporate business intercourse. These citizens are "artificial" in law and regulated as such. "Persons" must register and waive their home Nation rights and follow all the laws the host State has power to administer by statute and the 14th Amend. "Without,' or outside these Separate Powers is the Penumbra Doctrine which allows 'engraft' of 'subject citizens" to Maritime jurisdiction, and begat Admiralty, which drowned Equity.

Article I Congress only has power to "lay and collect taxes." The IRS violates its charter and the Separation of Powers by engrafting Article II police power at W-4 to collect the tax under devise of Maritime jurisdiction.

Black's. Commerce powers. Power of Congress to regulate commerce with foreign nations, and among the several states. Art. I Section 8, Cl. 3, U.S. Const.

Artificial citizen's corporate status is regulated by "public policy." Our rights are enumerated in the Bill of Rights and do not need Congressional approval. Vigilance is a requirement of each of the People to "declare" and maintain our "entitled" individual rights.

Black's. Expressum facit cessare tacitum. That which is expressed makes that which is implied to cease [that is, supersedes it, or controls its effect]. Thus, an implied covenant in a deed is in all cases controlled by an express covenant. Where the law sets down plainly its whole meaning the court is prevented from making it mean what the court pleases. Munro v. City of Albuquerque, 48 N.M. 306, 150 P.2d 733, 743.

The Bill of Rights is "express covenant" and protected by Article III Judicial and only "natural born Citizens" are "entitled" per Article IV Sec. 2 Cl. 1. Article I Legislative power is "implied covenant" and the state Citizen must have knowledge of the difference between these separate powers. Article I may only extend to its artificial subject citizens in corporate standing and statute rights obtained per agreement. The court cannot take away your rights, but you may waive all or part of them by contract with agency of Article II Departments, which "makes" police power to enforce dishonor.

Black's. Constitutional powers. The right to take action in respect to a particular subject matter or class of matters, involving more or less of discretion, granted by the constitution to the several departments or branches of the government, or reserved to the people. Powers in this sense are generally classified as legislative, executive, and judicial and further classified as enumerated (or express), implied, inherent, resulting, or sovereign powers… "Where Congress exceeds it authority relative to the States, therefore, the departure from the constitutional plan cannot be ratified by the 'consent' of state officials. An analogy to the separation of powers among the Branches of the Federal Government clarifies this point. The Constitution's division of power among the three Branches is violated where one branch invades the territory of another, whether or not the encroached upon Branch approves of the encroachment." New York v. United States (1992), 112 S.Ct. 2408, 120 L.Ed.2d 120.

The Governor of each state is responsible to the Constitutional Bill of Rights for the protection of its "natural born citizens." The governor cannot barter, sell the land or construct license to Thee People of "entitlement." State executive cannot interfere with Article III Judicial, for an 'inherent' class of citizen is domicile within. Though each state has leased space and jurisdictional forum to the federal government, the state Governor is bound to the Constitution regardless of "foreign" treaty. California Code 22.2.

"Just as the separation and independence of the coordinate branches of the Federal Government serves to prevent the accumulation of power in any one branch, a healthy balance of power between the States and the Federal Government will reduce the risk of tyranny and abuse from either front." New York v. United States (1992), 112 S.Ct. 2408, 120 L.Ed.2d 120.

Penumbra Double Speak

What is it, do you think, you thought I said? Is it my mind, that you think, you thought you read? Now your days will be filled with woe and dread, for it is the facts you should have gotten instead! William

TRUTH

The three conceptions of Truth are (1) Political and religious thought and reality at issue, the knowledgeable path and how to administer your individual affairs without liability to false teaching. (2) Generalship of the eventual verification of the issue, and Protection in your Personam of Law. (3) Statesmanship with consistency of thought within itself to defend the issued circumstance and teach Remedy.

Most of us are blissfully ignorant to the educational "social engineering" of Penumbra. We stumble into generalship without the Political knowledge required to represent our Personam to agency. The politician in us wants the peace of the statesman and we sign documents put before us "unconditionally," in the hope of fair play. Things happen and before we know it the bank is levying our account for the IRS or another "implied power." Penumbra agents can and do notify the work place of our "implied" debt, and besmirch our character to ruin after we volunteer the W-4 or like unit unconditionally. "Dishonor" is a "devise" of agency procedure found within the Uniform Commercial Code, and Credit of the People has been waived to a State forum of foreign jurisdiction. "Lawful money of the united States" has been displaced by "corporate America" Federal Reserve Accounting Unit Devise or FRAUD'S and Executive Maritime instrument of unconscionable nature. Because of this, We Thee People are limited in liability to the scraps of the aforementioned table OR, we must enable our individual "entitlements" to the Bill of Rights for Truth as intercede.

"An alien can exercise no political rights whatever; he cannot therefore vote at any political election, fill any office, or serve as a juror. Contracts in relation to the same - he is protected from injuries, and wrongs, to his person and property, his relative rights and character; he may sue and be sued. He owes a temporary local allegiance, and his property is liable to taxation."

The Political status of "artificial' 'persons" described in the 14th Amendment is presumptive adhesion to all state Citizens who do not reserve their rights. Any corporate agency or artificial "person" without consent of Thee Constitution cannot sue a Sovereign state Citizen. The People may only sue a state Citizen for probable cause of intentional crime.

The Immigration and Nationality Act is "a comprehensive federal statute embracing such matters as immigration, naturalization and admission of aliens. 8 U.S.C.A. 1101 et seq.

Political "persons' are from other Nations, or may have Maritime corporate status such as insurance agencies and are 'inhabitants" of Penumbra District. All "persons' are 'subject' to the jurisdiction of 'inferior courts,' which are answerable to Congressional and state Legislatures. Departmental standing per Article I Section 8 Clause 17 of the federal Constitutional forum guaranties are engrafts, and "subjects" are obligated under Article II Maritime jurisdiction.

The municipality, or corporation cannot sue a "state Citizen" without consent. We waive our Bill of Rights upon signing "unconditional' 'instruments" if we do not declare our "reservation" to the elliptical language contained within the document. No protest will review your voluntary in personam assent to "implied covenant" save revocation.

When the corporate "State of California' is a party, a contract of Maritime jurisdiction and waivers to Personam must exist to actuate Rule 12(b), and if you are lucky a little reasonable cause. When Thee People summon, there must be 'criminal intent," probable cause, victim and witnesses before a grand jury. Article III Judicial will only come to your aid when you are "entitled." The "People' must bind you to an Article III state Court instead of a District Court, of Article I and II Admiralty 'engrafted' 'implied Powers."

Through contract and waiver, the respective state "makes liable" those citizens who volunteer and do not call upon the "Express Covenant" as intercede. These contracts are constructed as waiver to Thee Sovereign Personam Jurisdictional Rights and add usurious conditions and Article I Statute court "rules of procedure' to seduce even the most vigilant to go before a 'subject matter' only 'inferior court,' 'engrafted" with Article II presumptive Maritime Jurisdiction.

Black's. Fourteenth Amendment. The Fourteenth Amendment of the Constitution of the United States, ratified in 1868, creates or at least recognizes for the first time a citizenship of the United States, as distinct from that of the states; forbids the making or enforcement by any state of any law abridging the privileges and immunities of citizens of the United States; and secures all" Persons" against any state action which results in either deprivation of life, liberty, or property without due process of law, or, in denial of the equal; protection of the laws. This Amendment also contains provisions concerning the apportionment of representatives in Congress.

I do not know whom these folks think they are kidding, but Article II Section 1 Clause 5 admits to the fact that there is a distinction between a "natural born Citizen' and a 'Citizen of the United States" in 1776. U.S. Citizen is described therein at Article I Section 8 Clause 17, and in the 14th Amendment as resident thereof in 1868. The U.S. Citizens were distinct from that of the state Citizens because they were "inhabitants' of the territories and remain 'resident' 'subject" status to this day. Statutes notwithstanding, all Citizens born within a state since the Constitution of 1776 were "natural born Citizens," including Dred Scott. Citizens born in territories were U.S. Citizens and became state Citizens upon statehood. Hawaii is the most recent, but the People do not know their status changed from U. S citizen to state Citizen. Civil Rights are intended for 14th Amendment corporate Citizens; diversity of Citizenship knows not what Nation "persons" are from, but what Liberties each enjoys under God and Constitution.

Amendment XIV [1868]. All persons born or naturalized in the United States, and subject to the jurisdiction thereof, are citizens of the United States and of the State wherein they reside. No State shall make or enforce any law which shall abridge the privileges or immunities of citizens of the United States; nor shall any State deprive any person of life, liberty, or property, without due process of law; nor deny to any person within its jurisdiction the equal protection of the laws.

"Subject to the jurisdiction thereof;" is totally under control of Fourteenth Amendment… All 'persons' are aliens, municipality, corporations etc., born, chartered or naturalized in the United States. US citizens, "municipalities and other government 'units' are 'persons' within meaning of 42 U.S.C.A. 1983," are all "UNCONDITIONALLY," controlled by contract within the residence of State, or the Congress and "are citizens of the United States and of the state wherein they reside." Aliens, corporations and municipalities only have one master; their allegiance required in a corporate charter. Aliens become "State" Federal citizens, and "subject" to Congress and the respective State at District law.

We the People are of state citizenship first, our second citizenship is to the United States. The "artificial citizen" must cling to Statute oath for citizenship rights. Those state Citizens who placed their political business into the hands of the wrong "maker' did so by the same 'take it or leave it" contract system, voluntarily. Citizens "made liable' as 'Persons" by statute may include a firm, association, municipality and other government departments of Penumbra. "Persons" are within the meaning of 42 U.S.C.A. 1983, corporation, legal representative, alien citizen and Agency activity contracted police powers.

"Civil rights ...are not connected with the organization and administration of government. Winnet v. Adams, 71 Neb. 817, 99 N. W. 681.

Yea and in California, a driver's license is not a contract, or so they say. Slavery, Dred Scott, Jim Crow laws, and the 14th Amendment are "connected with the organization and administration of government." We Thee People are entitled to our heritage, but our vigilance has given us to "eat scraps from the table" of the wrong master. Actually the cite is correct, civil rights are artificial liberties created by Congress for U.S. Citizens. We Thee People have been socially engineered into believing the Bill of Rights are "subject matter."

"Or as otherwise defined, civil rights are appertaining to a person in virtue of his citizenship in a state or Territory. Rights capable of being enforced or redressed in a civil action, which does NOT 'require criminal intent."

Civil rights are territorial and police power starts with in personam "dishonor" or "person of interest." The Bill of Rights protects preamble citizens of a state; police powers are not contracted but are activated with "probable cause" directed at your Personam. In personam jurisdiction of a state Citizen will stand only when a free person obligates and voluntarily becomes "made liable" by contract. Your signature on the issued license devise activates police power. Territorial civil rights "does not require criminal intent," only reasoned cause and the subject matter of Maritime jurisdiction. The contract or waiver is all that is needed to domesticate the state Citizen to "inferior" courts, and that deed has been accomplished in personam. Our state Bill of Rights and Article III have personam jurisdiction if criminal intent is proved. God created this body as Personam and I demurrer agency to remain a Freeman; otherwise signing unconditional contracts would take out parts and pieces of my spirit to worry, for I would be in slavery.

Civil rights is "also a term applied to certain rights secured to citizens of the United States by the 13th and 14th Amendments to the Constitution and various acts of Congress made in pursuance thereof."

The secured rights of subjects are civil and what is given as benefit may be taken away by greed, power, or Supreme Court brain freeze. The 13th and 14th Amendments prevent U.S. Citizens from being total slaves to the exact Maritime "public policy" system you are under at this writing. Article I "Inferior' courts, have 'made liable" the subject matter citizenship only unless we volunteer by signing a contract meant for them. The "natural born' are of enumerated Bill of Rights of the Article III

Judicial.   We are NOT 'MADE LIABLE,' unless by an in personam signature with one of the 'engrafted implied powers' which force compliance of the state Citizen by an 'unconscionable contract."

The ambiguous system of "units" are yokes of the People, for we are actually serving "two masters," but Penumbra will begin to chafe after your faith in TRUTH is Graced with wisdom of the "serpent." I reserve my Personam Rights prima facie upon any document I presume will waive any state Citizen Right, which are contained within "Thee Sovereign Covenant," I already have with God.

"Test for "ambiguous' is whether reasonable persons would find the contract subject to more than one interpretation. Tastee-Freeze Leasing Corp. v. Milwid, Ind.App., 365 N.E.2d 1388, 1390.

W-4 forms should have nothing to do with interpreting contract with your personal bank for failure to file.   I certainly did not give the state permission to raid my account, but they did and apparently with my permission.   Neither should IRS liens, or garnishments, but thanks to poor political knowledge, Penumbra binds all to the same forum system, unconditional contract of Maritime jurisdiction.   Article I Section 8 Clause 1; "Congress shall have power to lay and collect taxes." Article II maritime jurisdiction is collecting the tax.   Separation of Powers issue within Penumbra, and the scraps are thrown to "persons." "Active concealment" is what my ferret calls it.   This activity is Penumbra and avoidable even by contract with agency.

Signing our children into the forum public schools of "social engineering' to 'domesticate" their ideology instead of teaching knowledge should be the wake up call.   Personal body searches, testing of body fluids, zero tolerance without meaning or right, and police power to gang "sweep" schools without "criminal intent" of students are very serious acts of violated Trust and fairness.   Agency sends the message to our children, of how much sovereignty agency has and how "meek" the parenting must be if protective public policy procedures are "made" necessary by contract.   Your "required" signature upon any document should be avoided or representative of reserved Rights, which makes the unit "void on its face."

This "activity" may be estoppel on an individual basis by reserving your children's rights at the "registrar" signing or by addendum to your original instrument via certified mail.   Your child may then speak of God at commencement or rallies and sing in the choir without consent to search of their Personam.   Just say no!

Black's. A registrar is "an officer who has the custody and charge of keeping of a register. Person in educational institution in charge of registering students for enrollment."

A child's "enrollment," is as a "vessel," engaged in "home traffic" when occupying "other needful buildings." Unconditional parental assent to change citizenship from the state flag to the Federal Mast is complete. An Article III citizen has joined Article II Maritime jurisdiction to be "socially engineered" domestic product of public policy.

Black's. Petition. A written address, embodying an application or prayer from the person or persons preferring it, to the power, body, or person to whom it is presented, for the exercise of his authority in the redress of some wrong, or the grant of some favor, privilege, or LICENSE. A FORMAL written request addressed to some government authority.

State Citizens are not of corporate creation, yet our mail is addressed to a corporate Citizen, presumed under some duty to respond. Notice your name spelled in higher case, as letters from the IRS represent. Presentments are mailed in this manner to acknowledge covenant jurisdiction between one corporate "person" and your in personam being the other, not unlike a handshake.

The only way a state Citizen may rid his Personam of the corporate status is to refute its very existence with a reservation of Rights. You are the power, body, or person to whom the "prayer" was addressed. Your answer depends upon your generalship knowledge of agency forum. You are being "actioned," and your "authority" is needed at redress because you have the "privilege" of owning a ferret and it is wanted dead or alive, and you either give it up or tell agency why "public policy" cannot put you in jail for harboring such a hair ball.

A written answer is required "Without Prejudice" UCC 1-207 and agency is on formal notice that your property "entitlement' to 'privilege' and 'immunity" are not waived, voluntarily. Now the MPs must stay out of your play yard or stand ready to prove probable cause, with witness, other than the Executive State officer. No "crime" may be "actioned" without Thee Peoples knowledge and probable cause must be present. If your ferret gets arrested anyway, I want to know about it because "entitled" rights to a jury trial for controversy over $20.00 will trump ferret trapper any day.

The RIGHT of THE PEOPLE to petition for redress of grievance is guaranteed by the First Amendment, U.S. Constitution. Your child may be the only free spirit in their school to have their parent change the "consensual in personam jurisdiction" contract into one of Personam Liberty. An amendment to any contract changes the "unit" to non-negotiable as it adds a condition to an unconditional contract. Your personam signature is PROPERTY and the reservation separates the implied powers, so you may flee and "entitle" Thee Judiciary of Article III. This could be in the form of a U.C.C. 3-505, which kinda goes like this; the agent must have the unconditional certified authority to, grant, license, and subject matter, of the in personam "thing" in action at contract to proceed with "dishonor" process. Woe to you without your dictionary.

Black's. Indicia of title. Generally, document evidencing title to property, real or personal; e.g. carbon copy of bill of sale to automobile. Edwards v. Central Motor Co., 38 Tenn.App. 577, 277 S.W.2d 413, 416.

Allodial title and bill of lading are true titles, be wary of others, reserve Rights on questionable documents, couldn't hurt. Your pet ferret status must be changed to that of property and if this is all you learned from this treatise, bless your heart for saving the little nuisance. Nothing that teaches man kind love of fellow may be persecuted, unless it has taken your keys.

"An instrument on which is recorded, by means of letters, figures, or marks, the original, official, or legal form of something, which may be "evidentially" used. The term "document" applies to writings; to words printed, title-papers, receipts, and other written instruments used to prove a fact and used to support documentary evidence or authorities."

The "evidentially' 'mark" is your signature and it is definitely jurisdictional in any court. Evidence of participation in a joint venture of protective services and corporate power, whether it be unemployment, work comp., police or welfare is the unconditional signing. The "docket" starts as the "administrative record" and a reservation of rights will make the folder a lot smaller and your general has Personam flag.

A W-4, driver's license, bank account, co-op, work license, or receipt for a ferret is all property of the citizen at signing. An "explicit reservation of rights,' 'without prejudice" UCC 1-207, preserves your rights to such property under the Bill of Rights where criminal intent is required to obligate personam.

Indicia "within meaning of the best evidence rule, the document is any physical embodiment of information or ideas; e.g. a letter, a contract, a receipt, a book of account, a blueprint, or an x-ray. Strico v. Cotto. 67 Misc.2d 636. 324 N.Y.S.2d 483, 486.

Your reserved Rights scrawled as you will upon agency presentment enters here as "best evidence rule" before the trier of fact. The judge will not have the power to "certify" your obligation with a reservation to Rights of "entitlement" upon the instrument. A "reservation' binds the 'unit' to a 'CONDITIONAL' signing, and thereby voids 'Promise" of Negotiable Instrument Law at UCC 3-104(3), which vitiates police powers. This will stop the ferret hunters because your property rights prevent the "unit' from becoming a possession and subsequent 'contraband" at statute. The W-4 "without prejudice' UCC 1-207 and exempt, reserves your wage from "dishonor" as does other property by 'dilatory plea."

Black's. Dilatory pleas. A class of defenses at common law, founded on some matter of fact not connected with the merits of the case, but such as might exist without impeaching the right itself. They were either plea to the jurisdiction, showing that, by reason to some matter therein stated, the case was not within the jurisdiction of the court: or pleas in suspension, showing some matter of temporary incapacity to proceed with the suit; or pleas in abatement, showing some matter for abatement or quashing the declaration. Davis v. Thiede, 138 Ind.App. 537, 203 N.E.2d 835.

You "avoid' the 'words of art' 'invested' in 'implied powers' of Article I Statute 'subject' to 'inferior Courts' 'presumptuous' 'rule making," by reserving Rights. The Civil Procedures may ONLY sue an Article III citizen if he gives them permission, volunteers, waives or signs an instrument he knows full well is worthless to him and his children. I like the "QUASH" word because it voids negotiability of "unit."

Black's. Quash. To overthrow; to abate; to vacate; to annul; to make void; e.g. to quash an indictment.

This is what happens to civil laws, they break apart when we advise agency we are a diverse class of citizen and we do not wish to be "subject' to the same 'public policy' as an 'artificial subject matter" corporate citizen. This act does not make us different as Nation, but We Thee People are inherent. The Bill of Rights and the Article III Power of Judiciary are declarations of personam. Article I and Article II "implied powers" together cannot overtake the Supreme Court Judiciary.

Ambiguity, doubtfulness, double ness of meaning, or uncertainty of meaning of an expression used in a written instrument, is, in WANT of clearness or definitiveness. The instrument, a "subject matter" person signs is the same contract We Thee People stand in line, with children, ferret and the soldier, to covenant. These "persons' and other 'artificial municipalities' are 'subject' and 'required' to sign 'unconditional" instruments. We Thee people merely volunteer with a signing or waiver. We have not recognized the signing as a "meeting of the minds" and in good faith assent to the unconscionable language put before us. The bank has in its corporate subject matter, contract language of your "promise' to pay taxes, because understand this or not, you are of corporate status and 'domestic product." The signing gives the bank all it needs to levy your account for the sister State of "forum," I.R.S. Article I statute and Maritime jurisdiction, which is Article II and no Rights are violated. You volunteered!

Maybe there is no need to rush down to the bank, but put it on your list of things to do. Motor vehicles, school applications etc., give agency the "implied power' to 'presume' we have waived our 'personam' or personal rights. All this mischief makes for a bad handshake. Such action 'activity" takes place in Maritime jurisdiction. Subject matter and in personam jurisdiction at Rule 12(b) are certified and "make liable" all soldiers and "persons" of artificial creation.

We give agency permission to pry into Gods word for the elliptical blue smoke they think they have found to cover our eyes. Maybe that is why the lady at the courthouse is blindfolded. When we take the "New Covenant" path, that lady wont need the sword. Generalship is where that sword comes to play and We Thee People have the political savvy to bring all to Gods Law and Sovereign Covenant.

Thee People have just as much trouble in the mirror of the 14th Amend. The inferior courts assault on the Bill of Rights is more devise domestication than Law. The Bill of Rights stands untouched by civil rights. Civil Libertarian rights allow subject matter citizens to express their "actions" by using the Bill of Rights for only a few issues, which favor their defense. I think this is subterfuge to cover the overall subjugation of We Thee People into Maritime jurisdiction.

Black's. Artificial person. Persons created and devised by human laws for the purpose of society and the government as distinguished from NATURAL persons.

Corporations, Citizens born in Washington D.C., foreign residents and lawyers are examples of created persons. These "persons' are 'made' and 'liable' if their 'sworn' 'agency' duties do not follow proper statute procedure of their contract or dishonored promise to do or not to do a thing. Persons who are created by devise for the purpose of society and government, as distinguished from natural persons shows that Diversity of Citizenship would not be necessary if all persons were free, but alas some are subject and made liable to contract.

Black's. Artificial presumption. Also called "legal presumptions;" those which derive their force and effect from the law, rather than their natural tendency to produce belief.

In the old days "lex flatulent," I think the old dragon is very close. The engraft here is the "implied powers' of Article I and Article II, which 'makes' Admiralty Law, no matter how you scramble the words with police power or whatever fills the air. Agency does not need criminal intent from the "subject' person, for it is a 'thing" within its jurisdiction, does not possess personam and action may broadside at will. A produced belief that lies on presumption is sufficient as "subject matter' and 'personam" are waived in ignorance at signing.

Black's. Resident alien. A resident alien is a "person" within the meaning of the due process and equal protection of the Fourteenth Amendment. C.D.R. Enterprises, Ltd. v. Board of Ed, of City of New York, D.C.N.Y., 412 F.Supp. 1164, 1168.

When you sign contracts into the very same school, license, bank, and forums artificial citizens sign, then the same "domestic product" status applies to you and your children. The resident alien may only rely upon the 14th Amendment and there is no mention of Law or the Bill of Rights. Once again, the reason is because there are separate Citizenship Rights. Which would you prefer, taxes or ferrets?

Black's. In Personam. Against the person. The action in personam is that by which we sue him who is under obligation to us to do something or give something.

A personam right is your personal attachment to the Bill of Rights. In most issues the violation for which you are being 'held' (5th Amend.) had nothing to do with any of the Bill of Rights. Most are police power of Maritime instruments signed voluntarily. A state Citizen violation must be of "criminal intent" and indictable at probable cause, or you have waived your personam by contract. The same way the soldier voluntarily joins Admiralty. Subject matter persons do not have the right to personam jurisdiction. They are already liable by their negotiable presents and contracted to do business with the "masters" of court. Subject matter and in personam Maritime jurisdiction are all that is needed, to obligate school children, the alien citizen, ignorant state Citizen and the soldier at Rule 12(b). The school child and state Citizen share the same status, both waived Rights voluntarily, for "unknown benefit" and suffered the loss of their Sovereign Flag.

Black's. Subject Matter Jurisdiction. Term refers to courts competence to hear and determine cases of the general class to which proceedings in question belong; the power to deal with the general subject involved in the action. Standard Oil. v. Montecatini Edison S. p. A., D.C. Del., 342 F.Supp. 125, 129.

A soldier, alien, and corporate subject are of "general class" and the court must determine if the person can be tried under the statute before the court. The unprotected contract raises its ugly head to darkness once again. A right to "reasonable doubt" has been waived to represent "presumption of innocence' and 'information' as contrast to 'indictment." The "competence of a court is suspect and liable if it rules 'without right." The question before the court of being A.W.O.L., W-4 dishonor, ferret possession or truancy is answered with assent to negotiable instruments contained on the record as "facts of the subject matter stated." You and I are not soldiers, aliens, corporations or "subject," but the court will not know the difference unless you declare your flag. The courts "hearing' gets much better when we declare our entitlement of 'personam,' Preamble 'state Citizen' and not liable to any of the 'implied Powers' unless we assent to 'benefit" of protection.

The Federal Civil Judicial Procedure and Rules book, Rule 12(b). Defenses and Objections; (b) "…the following defenses may at the option of the pleader be made by motion: (1) lack of jurisdiction over the subject matter. (2) lack of jurisdiction over the PERSON… A motion making any of these defenses shall be made before pleading…(h) (3) "Whenever it appears by suggestion of the parties or otherwise that the court lacks jurisdiction of the SUBJECT MATTER, the court shall dismiss the action."

A court would not have jurisdiction if you would not sign unconditional obligations voluntarily. An Article I Brady Bill, Patriot Act, A.T.F., F.B.I., I.R.S., Courts Martial, or D.E.A. have jurisdiction over their subjects ONLY in an Article II "inferior court." A state citizen is entitled to "probable cause' with 'criminal intent" and warrant prior to arrest. Declaration of entitlement is issue of Article III, Judiciary. Actions for artificial persons are tried in the Article II court of Maritime jurisdiction, a state Citizen must have been "made liable" per dishonored instrument to be at action or assent tacitly. Both personam and subject matter issues are to be ascertained prior to "pleading," at the Administrative level. A court appearance all but assures jurisdiction if allowed to go that far without reserving your personam. "Without Prejudice' UCC 1-207 gives the court NOTICE that you are exercising 'REMEDY' available at the Common Law and the Code 'must' now be construed in 'HARMONY" with the Common Law at UCC 1-103.6.

Black's. Unconstitutional. When the legislation conflicts with some provision of our written Constitution, which is beyond the power of the Legislature to change. U.S. v. American Brewing Co., D.C.Pa., 1 F.2d 1001, 1002.

Congress must "make liable" its subjects, for this is a necessary function. The problem is, most of us get caught up in this "domestic war" and are surprised when our in personam is cuffed around our ankles. A court of foreign jurisdiction does not take kindly to the Constitution being brought up before their Mast. The Maritime beast will not survive a broadside of "Without Prejudice" UCC 1-207 for it strips her of police power and captures your state flag. The Common Law will find no crime and "adequate remedy of Law" must prevail or become unconstitutional on its face.

Article I Legislates "subject' matter for Federal Citizens with 'implied Powers,' 'Inferior Courts," and Admiralty brings the weaponry of enforcement. The big guns of the written Constitution are Thee Bill of Rights, and are in the image of Gods Law and TRUTH. Article III Judicial Powers are 'invested' in the 'Inferior' Courts of Article II Admiralty, because "persons" rights must not be violated, per contract.

UCC 1-207:3 Sufficiency of reservation. Any expression indicating any intention to preserve rights is sufficient, such as "without prejudice," "under protest," "under reservation," or "with reservation of all our rights." The Code states an "explicit" reservation must be made. "Explicit" undoubtedly is used in place of "express" to indicate that the reservation must not only be "express," but it must also be "clear" that such a reservation was intended. The term "explicit" as used in UCC 1-207 means "that which is so clearly stated or distinctly set forth that there is no doubt as to its meaning."

UCC 1-207:7 Effect of reservation of rights. The making of a valid reservation of rights preserves whatever rights the person then possesses and prevents the loss of such right by application of concepts of waiver or estoppel…

UCC 1-207:9 Failure to make reservation.

When a waivable right or claim is involved, the failure to make a reservation thereof causes a loss of the right and bars its assertion at a later date…

UCC 1-203:6 Common law - The Code is "Complimentary" to the common law, which remains in force except where displaced by the code.

A statute should be construed in harmony with the common law unless there is a clear legislative intent to abrogate the common law… "The Code cannot be read to preclude a Common law action."

Example: Your Honor, my use of "Without Prejudice UCC 1-207" above my signature on this document indicates that I have exercised the "Remedy" provided for me in the Uniform Commercial Code in Book 1 at Section 207, whereby I may reserve my Common law right not to be compelled to perform under any contract, commercial agreement, or bankruptcy, that I have not entered into knowingly, voluntarily, and intentionally. Reservation serves notice upon all administrative agencies of government national, state and local that I do not, and will not, accept the liability associated with the "compelled" benefit of any unrevealed commercial agreement.

Howard Freeman blazed this Liberty trail for We Thee People, he has passed on and our Lord will harvest the seeds he has sown.

Black's. Uniform Commercial Code 2-302 (1) If the court as a matter of law finds the contract or any clause of the contract to have been unconscionable at the time it was made the court may refuse to enforce the contract, or it may enforce the remainder of the contract without the unconscionable clause, or it may so limit the application of any unconscionable clause as to avoid any unconscionable result. (2) When it is claimed or appears to the court that the contract or any clause thereof may be unconscionable the parties shall be afforded a reasonable opportunity to present evidence as to its commercial setting, purpose and effect to aid the court in making the determination.

The W-4 instrument is the most unconscionable contract I never enjoyed signing, until I learned to sign with a condition, and now they think I am an ok Citizen, I think. The IRS is no different than ferret hunters in California, they go away upon notice that your personal property Rights are reserved, for agency forfeits police power and in personam Maritime jurisdiction.

D.C.Ga. 423 F Supp. 58, 61. Uniform Commercial Code.

A sovereign Citizen who does not recognize the corporate setting of their waiver to "inferior court' presumptive procedure may void their signature at personam subjugation to agency 'ab initio," due to fraud, duress and unconscionability. The Sovereign Citizen may force the court order a "clean bill."

States Citizen "entitlement" to Article III judicial is mostly waived by devise, fraud, duress or unconscionability. Personam is necessary to sever police action by signature or revocation on the voluntary obligation. The court has no choice but to dismiss or remedy in your favor, because no "satisfaction and accord" exist at unconscionable Maritime jurisdiction and you are entitled to judicial review.

Black's. Unconscionability. "Is generally recognized to include an absence of meaningful choice on the part of one of the parties, to a contract together with contract terms which are unreasonably favorable to the other party. Gordon v. Crown Central Petroleum Corp., the contract to have been unconscionable at the time it was made the court may refuse to enforce the contract, or it may enforce the remainder of the contract without the unconscionable clause, or it may so limit the application of any unconscionable clause as to avoid any unconscionable result. (2) When it is claimed or appears (presumptive) to the court (inferior) that the contract or any clause thereof may be unconscionable the parties shall be afforded a reasonable opportunity to present evidence as to its commercial setting, purpose and effect to aid the court in making the determination. UCC 2-302.

A W-4 is certainly unreasonably favorable to agency and once signed unconditionally, it becomes law between you, the IRS, bank, motor vehicle department, unemployment check, and you lose, voluntarily. In the old days an "exempt" on a W-4 would bring a $500 frivolous IRS police power "fact issue." "Without prejudice," severs the W-4 contract to state Citizens and slows down the rest. UCC 1-207 puts the burden on IRS, to prove you are "made liable' and since there is no certifiable Maritime instrument of negotiability, no obligation.

Corporate citizens are not exempt. We must not, nor should we waive our personam as vehicle to condition of employment or license. We Thee

People have made LAW an issue at Obligation of contract and have captured the flag of Admiralty. Facts of the subject matter, which we do not understand become issues of confusion by design and devise. We tend not to pay attention to elliptical details and "engrafted" language. All "implied" jurisdictions must be rebutted or dishonor will send us the negotiable end of police power.

A "government activity" is a "function of government in providing for its own support or in providing services to the public; e.g. taxation and the collection of taxes. Goble v. Zolot, 144 Neb. 70, 12 N.W.2d 311,312.

State of California "resident persons" 'provide for its on support" per Article I statute for their benefit and delict police power at will to "subject Citizens." A Sovereign state Citizen is entitled to the "privilege" and "immunities" enumerated within the Bill of Rights.

The collecting of taxes is "made" via the W-4 "Negotiable Instrument" which is LEGALLY capable of being transferred by enforcement of police power with delivery of "dishonor" to in personam subjects. When "providing for its own support" the government was obliged to recognize the above alien citizen for he "must" be "made liable" for the tax and other Penumbra agency that have the Jurisdiction to "engraft" this citizenship status. We the People have been dragged, kicking and screaming, even to the bank, to "UNCONDITIONALY" contract and "promise" Penumbra our rightful heritage, so everything is "fair and equal" for the support of government. The same liability is written into employment applications, un-employment, HMO, contractors license Etc. Churches, your parishioners may deduct their tithes. How wonderful for the government to provide the Church with tax "service" to enable their existence and non profit subject status. Agency made it so easy; your ignorance is hardly noticeable.

Now we see our political choice could have been made with much more care. Instead we visited ourselves grief, and the only alternative is generalship in Article II court, by our own hand. Your rights have not been violated because thus far all rights have been waived. Your activities are voluntary, as are those of the corporation or alien, no matter what the Penumbra; you are cleared for "Public Policy" Article II Law of Admiralty. Agency activity is Constitutional under the 14th Amendment, due process. You are treated equal with municipalities, corporations and other "artificial' 'persons" of subject matter jurisdiction. We The People have not lost a single Right, only waived them. We have assented to civil rights, police power of artificial municipalities and "persons," instead of declaring entitlement to the Bill of Rights and Article III Judiciary.

By the end of this writing you will understand that 42 U.S.C.A. 1983 is the venue to sue the individual agent or judge who does not follow his oath to the Constitution and uses "color of law" to obligate. When your rights have been waived, you are in personam "subject matter," and your activities are regulated and voluntary, as the good soldier and bad trapper.

Get out those dictionaries! First Amendment Study Team, a work in progress.

Black's. Make. To do, perform, or execute; as to make an issue, to make oath, to make a "presentment." To do in "form" of law; to perform with due formalities; to execute in "legal form;" as to make answer, to make a return or report. U.S. v. Giles, 300 U.S. 41, 57 S.Ct. 340, 344, 81,L.Ed. 493.

"Presumption" and "legal form" are to invent, presume, and imply. The citizen performs the obligation by oath and gets the bill one-way or the other. An unconditional signing under penalty of perjury makes an issue criminal in any court.

Blbs. Implied authority. In law of agency, power given by implied authority" being that which is necessary, usual and proper to accomplish or perform the main authority expressly delegated to an agent. Clark v. Gneiting, 95 Idaho 10, 501 P.2d 278, 280. principal to agent which necessarily follows from the express authority given though such power is not expressly asserted. Actual authority may be either express or implied, "implied authority" being that which is necessary, usual and proper to accomplish or perform the main authority expressly delegated to an agent. Clark v. Gueiting, 95 Idaho 10, 501 P.2d 278, 280.

After voluntary consent, a government activity agent has all the power he needs to terrorize the ignorant with his corporate police power. His next promotion may rely on how liable you volunteer to be. The entire system is built on this concept. The agent will use mailbox policy but must stop short of violating anyone's rights per agreement. After revocation of signature, the agent must avoid "color of law' 'liability," for the Sovereign Citizen may sue him in his own personal capacity.

Black's. Presumption. A presumption is a rule of law, statutory or judicial, by which finding of a basic fact, until presumption is rebutted. Van Wart v. Cook, Okl.App., 557 P.2d 1161, 1163.

If an agent were to presume you are "made liable" via presentment, would you know what to say? "Without prejudice" should be your response or you waive Rights of rebuttal, it is that simple.

Implied powers. "Such as are necessary to "make" available and carry into effect those powers which are expressly granted or conferred, and which must therefore be PRESUMED to have been within the intention of the constitution OR legislative grant." (cite omitted)

I smell bad air, again! Your citizenship and obligation instruments of all types are jurisdictionally implied in personam and subject matter is contracted to arrange police power and remedy for agency. But, see the part that says "constitutional' 'grant!" All you have to do is "ask and you shall be delivered," which is your clue to UCC'em,' do something! The agent may be slow, and get to the point of intimidation, but that is to our advantage. Reservation of rights abates presumption of compliance, and puts the burden of proving existence of obligation upon agent.

Article IV Section 2. (1) "The citizens of each state shall be entitled to all Privileges and Immunities of Citizens in the several states."

All natural, non-artificial persons are entitled to the same "inalienable" Rights to Article III and Bill of Rights, but we must "declare." We cannot surrender our Rights, BUT we may waive them. The state Citizen is privileged and immune from all Congressional Acts unless specifically named in the statute.

Black's. Inalienable rights. Rights, which are not capable of being surrendered or transferred without the consent of the one possessing such rights. Morrison v. State, Mo.App., 252 S.W.2d 97, 101.

There is a way to sever the "Penumbra" of commercial citizenship. Our courts work on presumption of your taking an equal liability for all civil law. A "preservation of Rights' is a contractual meeting of the mind at a "signing." That is your political nudge to protect the Right to contract. To have a valid contract, the essentials are (1) competent parties: Agency W-4, and a citizen of some sort who can "represent" himself or the corporation. A citizen must make the determination of how they wish to contract. You may sign "unconditionally" in personam, or Protect your Rights with a "Condition" that makes the signing an "unsigning" and may stand by your state flag with Personam intact. If you put a condition on the contract, agency cannot protest, for we have Rights not given to corporations. They "must take it or leave it."

A drivers license must allow your reservation upon the application, but do not wish for you to sign the representation on the license with your picture. Be meek, take the license home and find an indelible pen and reserve your rights above your signature. I put clear tape over the "dead in law" unit so the ink does not rub off. When the trapper sees the writing, he is on notice that my Rights are reserved.

When a signing takes place, there is a correctness or perjury statement at the bottom. This is your promise to follow the instrument to the very letter of it. When in your right mind, would you now sign a W-4 instrument without knowing the full body of "implied' 'presumptive' 'powers," contained therein? A marriage license looks very innocent, but it is a negotiable instrument, if you do not believe me ask any divorce lawyer.

The courts and their officers make good money from our own politically foolish contracts, which have "made liable" the people to agency. Bed counts are routinely made by local judges to make sure the proper amount of "persons" are sentenced to a jail facility, I think for the "implied power" and proprietary greed of the entity. Quite a profit, government maintains itself very well, the yoke for most, would not be so heavy if they would have began the signings, at the administrative level, with personal protective Rights. It is not too late to amend such contract by affidavit and notice of revocation via certified mail.

Signing "Without Prejudice" voids the "promise" at UCC 3-104.3 and perjury. A citizen cannot be actioned by any State without your own personal assent OR "criminal intent." Make them work for it, challenge Jurisdiction ALWAYS. Penumbra is "in want" of your Personam inalienable Rights.

I.R.S. Title 26 CFR 1-1.1-c Who is a citizen. (of the code) Every person born or naturalized in the United States and subject to its jurisdiction is a citizen.

Language of the 14th Amendment and Article I Territorial District is not nexus to the state citizen of Article III, but we may use their codes to vitiate obligation and control by statute without voluntary assent.

Let's have this phoenix "rise from the 'dead in law" file for just a bit and qualify. I stopped filing, dropped out, and drove without license, registration or insurance, I even own a ferret. I was not attending an accredited license school of "social engineering," because you cannot find this study discipline at such "negotiable" institutions. I can certainly see why! I have received summons of all like. Prior to my discovery of without prejudice, I stumbled into the same darkness you are in now; I "presume" that is why you are reading such a boring book on Law. The IRS visited my job and plucked me like the golden goose I promised I would be on the W-4. I tried every thing I could afford and decided to drop out. The government was at its best subjecting me to presentment facts of the IRS for years, because there is no statute of limitations for non-filing. I found it was not the facts of the IRS at dishonor, but the Law that created them.

I found I am "entitled" to be exempt, and may even sue my HMO without permission. At W-4 signing I represent Personam "without prejudice" UCC 1-207. No longer will my mind worry about what happens if I obligate to do or not to do a "thing," I can do as the free man I am and even have a ferret as my own personal property. My ferret has her own representation on her bill of sale, me. "Without prejudice" UCC 1-207 is a statement only the very ignorant public servant would ignore. If agent does, it is a personal excursion and will be very painful looking at a "1983" suit. I have heard the saying, "the only things that are sure in life are death and taxes." I defeated both with God's blessing, the Biblical "death" and taxes.

The W-4 signing is of a mutual benefit, wrong, government does not benefit by giving anything, sort of like the casinos in Las Vegas. Your unconditional W-4 gives license and permission to do, or not to do a thing. Duress and coercion do not make a good hand shake at contract. Only a "subject' 'must,' sign as 'offered" and the document is then "authenticated" as being under the jurisdiction of Article II Maritime jurisdiction and statutes apply.

Black's. License. Permission by competent authority to do an act which, without such permission, would be illegal, a trespass, or a tort.

I am sure you would be surprised to learn that very few licenses are required under the common law. Those who have license to practice anything, drive, or fix boilers, may protect your property as license with a reservation of your natural Rights. A statute claiming to have power over a "subject" who does something that is "illegal" should not represent to the natural Citizen that the issue is unlawful. We give the IRS "permission by competent authority" to do something that would be illegal otherwise, when we sign the W-4 unconditionally. The Citizen gives IRS license to in personam jurisdiction by signing the W-4 Maritime instrument unconditionally.

Black's. Offer. "A promise to perform is inferred if the offeree commences the undertaking."

You are the one who fills out a contract and "commences the undertaking" of the W-4 whether required or not. Agency's "infer" you will follow the statutory procedure prescribed and expectation must meet the terms or police power is activated. Presumption is all over the place. Problem is we never rebut the "inference" that a presumption exists. Helmet laws, jaywalking, selling personam firearms, dog license, and ferrets are illegal and considered contraband at "possession," but not unlawful as property. These are adhesion contracts to your "registered" in personam and expectation of assent may be rebutted, which is a rare declaration by the entitled Citizen. Paying tax, seatbelts and the like are adhesions to present license, but are "inferred." Neither the IRS nor trapper is a "giant" and exist as such by your voluntary compliance to duress and police power.

When your ferret is spotted by the tracker in your front yard, he cannot corrupt with blood the poor thing until you sign an agreement to terms of action, via summons. Firmly grip a writing instrument and scribe "without prejudice" UCC 1-207 upon the devise above your signature. Presentment or summons may follow the intrusion upon your gate, and this is another opportunity to reserve the Rights to use your Personam property. You become in personam if you fail to answer or sign the instrument unconditionally and the process will continue until the final day. You license agency to use police powers to "take" by devise, your unauthorized pet as contraband. Don't wait for a vote or petition, protect your property, and reserve it for Personam use only. The trapper will not come into your yard, the agent must have probable cause and warrants are required.

Black's. Presumption. In ALL civil actions and proceedings not otherwise provided for by Act of Congress or by these rules, a presumption imposes on the party against whom it is directed the burden of going forward with evidence to rebut or meet the presumption, but does not shift to such party the burden of proof in the sense of the risk of nonpersuasion, which remains throughout the trial upon the party on whom it was originally cast. Federal Evidence Rule 13.

I am not at all sure you got that so I will presume to "imply" it. A civil action is an "artificial issue' with 'Implied Powers" as force of police action at "dishonor" of promise. Acts of Congress cannot provide rules of procedure for the citizen of Article III; those are inalienable and scribed Thee Ten Amendments. Rights enumerated in the Bill of Rights are already in place; all your Personam must do is "declare entitlement."

Agency makes presentment and we have the burden of going forward with evidence of our not being "made liable." The best proof is prima facie upon the original unit and you demand certified signature of obligation. A unit with reserved Rights prima-facie cannot be used as evidence in a Maritime jurisdiction tribunal, lest agency forget Rule 12(b).

Reserve your rights and remember a state citizen cannot be sued unless he assents. Agency may impose obligations presumptively and you are not guilty until proven innocent in Maritime jurisdiction. When the Citizen refutes the issue, he trumps the burden of proof to agency. It is a violation of Law if you are "subject" and fail to perform as promised. Where do we get the evidence that we do not owe a duty? Many attorneys later, we find we can rebut without proof or attorney because we shift the burden to agency, with assent of a conditional signing or "without dishonor." State citizen rights "must" be construed in "harmony" with Code Law under the Bill of Rights and Article III. UCC 1-103.6, and the "adequate remedy at Law" will stand.

This remedy will abate the issue, or "deliver" the wolf to the Truth of a 1983, "color of law" action. When you cannot predict contractual outcome of Federal Maritime jurisdiction, protect the Rights of your state Flag and Article III with Personam declaration. Go California! Your state becomes your State when you contract with State Departments of Federal forum statutory creation, as subjects are required to do. The 14th Amendment due process of police powers and units of dishonor, are of Maritime jurisdictional obligations, and voluntarily assigns capture of your state flag upon unconditional signing. Agency failed to disclose this Penumbra as part of your subjugation and you have the Right to revoke the negotiability of the unit at any time. Fraud cannot hide behind "color of law" and non disclosure.

Black's. In propria persona. In ones own proper person. It was formerly a rule in pleading that pleas to the jurisdiction of the court must be plead in propria persona, because if pleaded by attorney they admit the jurisdiction, as an attorney is an officer of the court, and he is "presumed" to plead after having obtained leave, which admits the jurisdiction.

Personam is your treasure of Rights which was created as a temple for God to judge the sins of it. Propria persona is your Personam, standing before the court and challenging jurisdiction over your person to obligation presented by agency. Reality of Truth gives authority to speak, but silence is best until the adversary has been delivered. My Personam dares not make a step or sign a contract without Counsel. Jesus warned about lawyers and he speaks with "authority."

Penumbra has retained lawyers who use statutory procedures and translate Executive Maritime jurisdiction as an "officer of the court." Have no fear of these guys unless you rely on even one to know Law. When the lawyer files papers with the court, you are no longer Personam, but in persona because you have agreed to terms per instrument devise and the lawyer is "standing in your stead." The state Citizen must plead in his own state Citizen person.

Only a sovereign citizen may enter a plea in a common law court or with "competent state counsel." All pleas by the sovereign Citizen must challenge the jurisdiction over his PERSONAM or state citizenship person and the subject matter. Remember, an "artificial person" is a creature of State origin, and has no PERSONAM for juristic notice. An attorney knows only subject matter procedure and cares not about personam. He does not know Law and is an artificial citizen and cannot plea to the common law.

He can only represent others of his corporate status who hire him to "stand in their stead." Lawyers are Executive forum officers of Maritime jurisdiction.

Only a state citizen may represent his or her protected rights of in propria persona. I have not been to courts recently, for I find them respectful of the UCC at the common Law, even from a distance. Agency is very well advised of my contracting Rights. Now comes the Citizen of Personam "de bene esse" by certified mail, I do not go to court for it is alien to the Common Law and I have no nexus at Mast. The courts have never answered any of my mail, proclivity of your adversary is for no answer at all, and I consider the issue a win and seek knowledge of why.

The court presumes you are guilty, and after a quick look to see if everyone is insured, it's off to "public policy" ranch. Of course all this went on because you waived your common Law Rights. Summary judgment will come quicker, if you nod your head up and down real fast. With trembling chains waive speedy trial, and the pirates will have your silk purse and a warrant for your pearls. The "negotiable' and 'presumed' artificial in personam is in proprietary confinement under 'color of contract' extorted by engraft to your state via Article I Statutes and Article II 'forum." The proceedings are civil and you gave your negotiable Personam to tribunal by de facto devise, police power and waiver. A well-placed Affidavit will challenge jurisdiction at the administrative level and works wonders for your proper personam status. When I reserve MY Rights, agency is notified; I AM, not intending to smother with facts, but to consume with Truth.

Black's. Affidavit. A written or printed declaration or statement of facts, made voluntarily, and confirmed by the oath or affirmation of the party making it, taken before a person having authority to administer such oath or affirmation. State v. Knight, 219 Kan. 863, 549 P.2d 1397, 1401.

Now this is where the Truth is apparent. First of all a sovereign citizen needs no Law of notary at Deuteronomy 19:15 for the purpose of establishing "notice" of our intention to de-foliate their garden of dragon food. We give unconditional signature under penalty of perjury, which makes an excellent "declaration" and conveniently easy to "confirm," when written upon the instrument at issue.

A judge or artificial person "must" jump through many hoops of implied power before the ferret dies, go now and make that baby a property issue. We Thee people are of Judiciary power and neither Article I, nor Article II, with all their implied powers and engraft can breach our "Sovereign Covenant" of inheritance and Capture Flag. The voluntary, unconditional signing of a W-4 under perjury will be before the judge also as in personam jurisdiction, per Rule 12(b); I pray your Rights are reserved prima facie upon it.

Black's. Presentment. Presentment is a DEMAND for acceptance or payment made upon the maker, acceptor, drawee or other payor by or on behalf of the holder. UCC 3-504.1.

The presentment is to be taken very seriously and answered quickly. If the citizen ignores the instrument, ticket, summons, or 30-day notice it becomes negotiable, because you have "dishonored" a "unit" demand for payment under UCC 3-504(1) after you promised to appear. I have used the following "rebuttal" to a debt I did not owe, and it has never failed me. On the instrument, prima facie I write, "I hereby refute the validity of your unattested presentment/claim of action, 'without dishonor,' I do not owe this money' 'Without Prejudice" UCC 1-207. Send the instrument to the individual agent as soon as possible, via certified mail, dated and signed. Do not trade barbs with collection agents over the telephone; force agency to mail you presentment, or facts of the matter stated. A couple of times the agency has sent again the instrument, usually from another agent, and I again respond. This time with a UCC 3-505, which states; "In order to protect himself, the party to whom presentment is made may require the following without thereby dishonoring the instrument." A copy of such form can be found within this writing. ONLY demand the information enclosed therein. It is a demand for the debt instrument containing your signature, without prejudice denies the instrument life and police power which makes the unit "dead in law." Someone "must," sign under penalty of perjury that instruments of debt exist and proof must be certified by trier of fact before warrant shall issue. The agent must furnish reasonable identification. The Common Law sues the individual agent and not the "whole world." Direct correspondence to a person if possible, the IRS usually does not put names on their presentments, but the paper work will have traceable numbers on them in case a John Doe is needed.

Black's. Commercial law, Presumption. A presumption means that the trier of fact "must" find the existence of the fact presumed unless and until evidence is introduced which would support a finding of its non-existence. UCC 1-201(31).

What "trier" needs to hear is an affirmation of Truth as a rebuttal. No fact of debt exists if rights are reserved upon the instrument. Without prejudice is an "affirmative defense" and notifies agency of your "entitlement" to state citizenship and Article III Bill of Rights. The burden of proof has been rebutted for implied powers of agency to prove the assumption of debt, claim, or use of police power. We know by now that implied means presumptive, but stands as a fact of Law unless rebutted. A natural Citizen has no need to prove the fact of his personam. An artificial person "must" appear in the inferior Courts of Article II Maritime jurisdiction in personam. We Thee People are blessed with assenting directly to The Law of God and Article III Judicial to redress our grievance of Law.

Black's. Without Prejudice. Where an Offer OR Admission is made "without prejudice," or a motion is denied or a suit dismissed "without prejudice," it is meant as a DECLARATION that NO RIGHTS of the party concerned are to be considered as thereby waived or lost. (Emphasis added).

Your personam will be reserved and entitled. When your state Citizenship Right to be heard is waived in law, you must appear in the proper Admiralty court of statutory procedure, per dishonored contract.

Black's. Declaration. The declaration, at common law, answers to the "libel" in ecclesiastical and admiralty law, the "bill" in equity, the "petition" in civil law, the "complaint" in code and rule pleading, and the "count" in real actions.

The term "complaint" is used in the federal courts AND in all states that have adopted Rules of Civil Procedure.

"It may, however, be considered settled that letters or admissions containing the expression in substance that they are to be "without prejudice" will NOT be admitted in evidence… an arrangement stating the letter was without prejudice was held to be inadmissible as evidence… not only will the letter bearing the words, "without prejudice" but also the answer thereto, which was not guarded, was inadmissible…" Ferry v. Taylor, 33 Mo. 323; Durgin v. Somers, 117 Mass 55, Molyneaux v. Collier 13 Ga. 406. (Emphasis added).

The "declaration" answers agency with a Wall of Law, irrefutable notice of "entitlement." An agent would be a fool to action "color of Law" to force the obligation without voluntary assent. Notice how Law explains itself; whereas facts are anything the "maker" of the implied power "presumes" it to be and with our poor politics, we have lost many a ferret to "public policy." "Without Prejudice," accomplishes the following; no evidence, perjury, promise to appear, W-4, 1040 filing, writing, or statement can be held against you. A grand jury cannot hear a cause without a Citizen of a state as victim at "criminal intent," which invokes entitlement to Article III Judicial. Only if probable cause of a crime exists, does "true bill" and warrant issue from Thee People. The State of California is a Commercial venture of Executive forum at Article II, and may only bind federal citizens in their "resident" State via Admiralty devise. You make "declaration" as entitlement to Thee Bill of Rights and agency flag is yours.

Black's. Residency requirements. Broad term to describe terms of residence required by States for such things as welfare benefits, admission to the bar, divorce, etc.

When you contract with Maritime equity, expect only equity in return. You are either a state Citizen with permanent "domicile" or "resident" lawyer of State and subject to tax. Your statement of fact to these entities, are contractual issue of law and Citizenship status is very important. The promise to pay the tax and to be "subjected" to agency police power is contained elliptically within the negotiable unit of Penumbra. Your rights cannot be violated, because you had a meeting of the minds concerning the matter stated, and you signed voluntarily. You have just sworn on your license, permit, ticket, tax statement, W-4 form, jury summons, and the ferrets' life that you are an "artificial U.S. citizen" and subject matter regulations apply, because you have waived your personam rights. That is until you REBUT, "Without Prejudice" UCC 1-207. Sign the instrument and enjoy whatever rights you then possess. The license, summons, or ticket is tainted as NON-NEGOTIABLE and "without dishonor," just in case agency has a problem with your compliance. After my signing without prejudice UCC 1-207, my rights may be violated if the agency attempts to raise the "dead in law" instrument to the courts for "color of Law" decision and negotiability.

When correspondence had commenced "without Prejudice" but afterwards those words were dropped, it was immaterial; 6 Ont. 719. The term "admission" is usually applied to civil transactions and to those matters of fact in criminal cases which do not involve criminal intent, while the term "confession" is generally restricted to acknowledgments (waivers) of guilt. People v. Sourisseau, 62 Cal.App.2d 917, 145 P.2d 916, 923.

Agency "must' prove probable cause at the administrative level, prior to court; because this is where Article III supercedes any and all Article II implied power. Judicial Power is not implied, but guaranteed to the entitled Preamble Citizen and but, Rights must be declared. Article II agency cannot sue Article III Citizen civilly unless a negotiable unit has been executed.

A statement is not hearsay if the statement offered against a party is (A) his own statement, in either his individual or representative capacity, or: The truth is in the signing; your representation of "without prejudice" is intended as a DECLARATION. (B) A statement of which he has manifested his adoption or belief in its truth. Without prejudice is a direct assault on agency facts and presumptional "information," makes the issue a matter of Law, without prejudice as to TRUTH and belief. Remember, an attorney is an Executive officer of the court, as is the judge, both are bias and neither are "competent counsel" for the state Citizen.

Access to Article III cannot be done with an attorney; he is civil, corporate, and "standing in your stead," unless he is of state law counsel and I have not found this "honorable man." Without prejudice, will serve notice on any judge that the presumptive court is in "want' of jurisdiction over your 'personam" and you are declaring your entitlement. Burden of proof reverts to agency unless they have a "valid' claim, which would be automatic, over the artificial 'persons' for its 'domestic product" purpose. Remember agency charter "must' be under 'the jurisdiction thereof" the 14th Amendment of contracted agency control or the presumption of claim will not stand. A sovereign Citizen has the first Ten Amendments as Law of his New Covenant, IF, he has Rights reserved.

Common Law dictates, the UC code is "Complementary" to the common law (UCC 1-103.6) which remains in force except where displaced by the code… a statute should be construed in harmony with the common law unless there is clear legislative intent to abrogate the common law… the code cannot be read to preclude a common law action." "Without prejudice," or a motion is denied or a suit dismissed "without prejudice," it is meant as a declaration that no rights or privileges of the party concerned are to be considered as thereby waived or lost except is so far as may be expressly conceded or decided.

This story is getting better and better. UCC 1-207 is a "declaratory" relief demand and you have exercised "Remedy" and entitlement at the common Law. You have also "abated' or challenged the jurisdiction of agency police power. A court cannot continue without a "negotiable instrument," and agency is "in want' of jurisdiction. "Notice has been given to the 'artificial persons' on the receiving end of the above stated entitlement. You have successfully made your political and religious status known. The court "must' now administer the Common Law, which does not exist for the 'artificial" person. Doesn't it make sense that a natural person would have more rights than an "artificial person?" Makes sense or not it is Thee Law of Thee Land.

UCC 1-207.3 Sufficiency of reservation. An expression indicating ANY intention to preserve rights is sufficient, such as "without prejudice," "under protest," "under reservation," or "with reservation of all our rights."

UCC 1-207 means "that which is so clearly stated or distinctly set forth that there is no doubt as to its meaning." By now you realize you are entitled to inalienable Rights and know you must declare those rights to agency as reservation Notice. If you have unconditionally signed an unconscionable contract, you may rescind or revoke any contract that failed to disclose the Citizenship diversity and police power devise hidden within.

We Thee People must "Capture Flag" or suffer the yoke of its inferior courts and go before the Masted Admiralty. If we do not declare our Rights of heritage in Truth of Law, We Thee People will lose "entitlement" to even rebut "dishonor."

Black's. Offer. The offer CREATES a POWER of ACCEPTANCE permitting the offeree by accepting the offer to TRANSFORM the offeror's promise into a CONTRACTUAL OBLIGATION. (Emphasis added).

By signing an agreement unconditionally, you "create a power of acceptance" to the "implied power" agency that you waive your rights to Article III Judiciary and you will stand before the Mast when summoned. By lowering your state Citizenship Flag voluntarily, you have exposed your Personam to a broadside of Admiralty and assented to its capture. You give agency police powers and subject yourself to "reasonable cause" and must obligate through devise. You are now a commercial "artificial person" of Article I-8-17 creation and "must" assent to the rules of Article II forum Maritime jurisdiction, even as they may change wiggly-wiggly. Agency has no choice but to accept your conditional instrument, although they may wiggle the pigly, just a little. An agent may ask what the phrase means, but no answer will help, not usually anyway. Just say "Rights Notice," and go mute. You are neither a barrister, nor "knowledgeable in the Law" and are "without Competent Counsel" and "wish to remain silent" and await the Grace of proclivity.

You're W-4, work license, bank, schools, marriage license, etc. are offers, and you have the Right to "Obligation of Contract" that will bind agency with Thee representative of YOUR Choice. Assent "unconditionally" at your own peril.

A Miranda warning would qualify as an offer, because it is an admission and understanding to the jurisdiction of the court and may be avoided by reserving your Rights prima facie. You have the right to remain silent. A "tacit" admission of jurisdiction, with an attorney represent, or not, will begin the procedure of Statute subject matter codes of Maritime jurisdiction.

Silent means completely silent, if agency puts paperwork before you, sign "WITHOUT PREJUDICE" UCC 1-207 above your signature. A whole new world of Law will raise from the very ashes agency wishes it would lay. Remain SILENT. Anything, I mean ANYTHING you say CAN and WILL be USED against you in a court of State Statute Admiralty. SILENT!

You have the right to have an attorney present before being questioning if you desire. When you assent to attorney, you waive your Bill of Rights because, an "artificial person' is "acting" in your personam and 'proper forum" and procedure of summary justice will prevail. If that does not do the trick, then answer yes to the following engagement from court. Do you understand the charges? A "yes' is 'tacit' admission that you are waiving personam jurisdiction to the court. You have admitted an Article I statute exist and is at issue, and you have notice of an obligation to perform a duty. Only Statute subject matter needs to be heard.

In police work an "interview" is performed pre Miranda. If an Interrogation or QUESTIONING is needed then Miranda "must" be given. They are TRICKY. SILENCE, use the codes and Article III as Rebuttal and declare entitlement, Remedy at Article III. Our state has done everything BUT admit to the District courts of Admiralty's presence in Thee Peoples Courts. The UCC may actually be used to terrorize agents who cannot see, are stone deaf, or touch your ferret.

Black's. Magistrate. The term in its generic sense refers to a person clothed with power as a public civil officer, or a public civil officer invested with Executive (Article II) or Judicial Power (Article III). Ex parte Noel, Ky., 338 S.W.2d 903, 907.

A person clothed with power as officer invested with Executive Article II or Judicial sounds as though the wolf has taken many sheep. "Clothed" any kind of "officer" is statute Maritime jurisdiction. Look at the flag near the judge, is it Masted or of your Sovereign state. Think quickly because your new master awaits his offering.

Implied power begat presumptive facts and there were evidence of sow's ear everywhere; the horror! All "persons" were submissively standing in long lines and waiting to nod their heads up and down by signing unconscionable agreements with agency. MPs were everywhere, arresting "persons of interest" and "gang sweeping" the schoolyard. The children could not talk of God and the X Commandments was delict from the courthouse. Their flag was distorted with gold as if bought and the borderlines between its states had been erased. The Peoples Flag had been captured by devise, yet Loyalty of its Citizens prayed to public policy and waived Rights to the Law of the Land. They had not heard of God going before them, to do the fighting. All they had to do was pray that their leaders would guide them as a Nation and God will intercede and lead. The future of this nation must be dependant on God or We Thee People are just another sow's ear generation. Posterity is not gotten without salted herb on your politics and the Lamb is in the field. Facts will not fill His cup and woe to yea who covenant falsely to worry; your soul may be forfeit, if your nakedness hides Truth.

"It is an elementary rule of pleading, that a plea to the jurisdiction is… a "tacit" admission that the court has a right to judge in the case, and is a waiver to all exceptions to the jurisdiction." Girty v. Logan, 6 Bush Ky. 8.

A tacit plea is silence or a YES to understanding the charges put forth in an action, "information," summons, or if you did not represent yourself "without prejudice." A YES to understanding the charges evokes jurisdiction as will showing up with or without attorney. The court may go forward, because you understand you have not paid your tax or obtained the proper "Public Policy" license, or have a contraband ferret in your possession. My signature is PROPERTY within the meaning of ARTICLE III, and an unconscionable signing of agency statute may be voided at the administrative level. Article II forum Admiralty does not have police power without contract.

Black's. Tacit. Existing, inferred, or understood without being openly expressed or stated, implied by silence or silent acquiescence, as tacit agreement or a tacit understanding. State v. Chadwick, 150 Or.645, 47P.2d 232, 234. Done or made in silence, implied or indicated, but not actually expressed. Manifested by the refraining from contradiction or OBJECTION; inferred from the situation and circumstances, in the ABSENCE of EXPRESS MATTER...

Sounds like more elliptical breathe of the old Penumbra Dragons sow's ear section. I surely hope you can see the fog before it gets to your nose. What you do say, what you do not say or what is inferred you didn't say or said or if you just get it wrong. Without prejudice would be the contrary cause or Dilatory Plea or OBJECTION, which raises the RIGHTS issue; unless you are like most, nod your head up and down, get in line and obligate. ONLY YOU have enumerated, and guaranteed entitlement to the Bill of Rights and Article III as intercede, which is in perfect HARMONY with the UCC, and is an "EXPRESS MATTER."

Black's. Express. Clear; definite; explicit; plain; direct; unmistakable; not dubious or ambiguous. Declared in terms: set forth in words. Directly and distinctly stated. Made known distinctly and explicitly, and not left to inference. Minneapolis Steel & Machinery Co. v. Federal Surety Co., C.C.A.Minn., 34 F2d 270, 274. Manifested by direct and appropriate language, as distinguished from that which is inferred from conduct. The word is usually contrasted with "implied."

This is Common Law language, without the Dragon Flatulent. "Without Prejudice" is such word of Truth and Thee Master of them will Grace its use. When 'declared' directly,' 'explicit,' 'unmistakable' and 'not left to inference' you may see the 'contrast' between Penumbra forums of government which 'imply" power and Thee Bill of Rights. When "inferred" conduct is taken as fact; you missed your chance to reserve rights because your head was nodding up and down in voluntary compliance. The inferred becomes fact and the magistrate may now certify your dishonor of a negotiable instrument. Garnishment and lien follow with the police power you "granted" upon the W-4 instrument. When the people use unconditional equity, police power is de jure. When police power is upon the state Citizen, it is de facto without contract and "in color of law." An entitled state Citizen may wear their individual state flag as a robe when Rights are reserved. A Federal court colors must unmast or loose its flag to the Citizen.

Black's. Tacit admission. An acknowledgment or concession of a fact INFERRED from either silence or from the substance of what one has said. (Emphasis added).

When "words of art" are present in an instrument, their claim is for real "things" of "negotiability." Your "domestic product" will do just fine in jail because the government will not take a loss in having your children in foster care, and replacing your job with someone equally as vigilant as we have been. You're home repossessed, property "taken" without right, ferret impounded and for what; a "tacit" acceptance of implied law. Belief in Article II Statutory system of "due process" is a "ping" to Admiralty from ignorance.

We Thee People are not soldiers who "must" waive personam Sovereignty Rights. Article III and Thee Bill of Rights must not to be taken lightly by agency, which must follow public policy UCC. Amendment V, "without due process of law," is for the Citizen of the state, wise enough to part his personam from the subject matter of the "NEGOTIABLE" contract. Amendment XIV, "without due process of law,' is for 'artificial citizens' 'subject to the jurisdiction thereof,' 'the United States and the State wherein they reside." Law, which represents the "artificial persons,' is of corporate Maritime jurisdiction and the sovereign Citizen has no 'business" in those courts, unless they are seeking equity as the good soldier.

UCC I-207: 7. Effect of RESERVATION of rights; The making of a "valid" reservation of rights PRESERVES WHATEVER rights the person then possesses and prevents the loss of such right by application of concepts of waiver or estoppel… (Emphasis added).

Even if you were an artificial person, the statute must now follow proper procedure of the dedicated "charter" of agency, AND a negotiable contract must exist in dishonor. You may have signed the negotiable instrument and are now "avoiding" the consequences of the act. You definitely should not waive to contrary "words of art' or 'arbitrary and capricious" obligation. Rules of another's court are more the reason to remain silent. There is no implied power that can force you to defend yourself against statute. An attorney can do this successfully, but he has a sow's ear for you to sign unconditionally, and he will be very bias, after all he has a job to protect, and when lawyer is present, in personam jurisdiction is complete.

SILENCE, you are "not knowledgeable in the Law' and are 'in want of competent counsel," I know I repeat myself, BUT, pay attention. This Individual sovereign can have no "court officer" appointment. The District Attorney must be appointed by the Governor to promulgate the executive in a Common Law action per state Common Law at California Code 22.2. The Judge "must" be elected by Thee People to represent the Article III, Bill of Rights. There "must' be a victim and a Grand Jury Indictment at Amendment V.

Avoid "information" at all cost, an answer of "without Prejudice," assures justice, if you remain vigilant and answer all presentments with a representation of Rights. Facts are confusing and varied; Law will fight for you, if the proper court is convened.

Black's. Valid. Having legal strength or force, executed with proper formalities, incapable of being RIGHTFULLY over thrown or set aside

Maritime jurisdiction requires in personam and subject matter or dismissal under Rule 12(b). A Personam signing of without prejudice enables the unit and makes it "incapable of being rightfully over thrown or set aside," and vitiates promise. The W-4 has the same "legal strength and force" when signed unconditionally under penalties of perjury. The valid instrument will be jurisdictional fact, on the administrative record and may be executed to the fullest extent of the agreement. There is no petition, protest march, or tort action which will interfere with Tribunal and "Obligation of Contract." We Thee People must declare our Citizenship or lose our Separate Article III "entitlement" power when contracting propria persona.

Black's. Made. Produced or manufactured artificially. U.S. v. Anderson, D.C.Cal., 45 F.Supp. 943, 946. To have required or compelled. Dickinson v. Mingea, 191 Ark. 946, 88 S.W.2nd 807, 809.

The IRS "privacy act' is notice, and "persons 'made liable' are required to file a '1040 or a tax statement." First thing was to find what "made liable' means and to which extent obligated. I knew a contract must exist or an action could not be certified to force contractual demand to file 1040 or statement. The W-4 is the gateway to Title 26, a five-inch book on factual legal terror. A conditional writing of without prejudice, on the unconscionable unit, results in non-assumpsit and declaration of entitlement to the common Law, and matters not who "made" the instrument.

Black's. Liable. Obligated; accountable for or chargeable with. Condition of being bound to respond because a wrong has occurred. Condition out of which a LEGAL LIABILITY might arise. Pacific Fire Ins. Co. v. Murdoch Cotton Co., 193 Ark. 327, 99 S.W.2d 233, 235. (Emphasis added).

Somewhere there is something I missed while fighting facts of agency. Facts and presumptions become Law if not rebutted! I recalled past uses of without prejudice and discovered agency did not proceed very far after my reservation of rights. I knew I was worth the trouble, so something was coming into view. Agency could not force an unconditional signing and without prejudice UCC 1-207 vitiated the unconscionable unit, and agency lost police power with the same stroke of Thee Word. I looked at what operated the agency and supplied its rules of charter, I found the Negotiable Instruments Law and the codes the agency "must" follow and BAM, instant success at unconditional signing at UCC 3-104.2. Reality is powerful when the Truth of elliptical forum reveals its secrets. Facts of IRS are meant to draw your attention from the real issue, Law of contracting.

Black's. Standing to sue doctrine. The requirement of "standing" is satisfied if it can be said that the plaintiff has a legally protectable and tangible interest at stake in the litigation. Guidry v. Roberts, La.App. 331 So.2d 44, 50.

As soon as I started my next job, I signed a W-4 "Without Prejudice" UCC 1-207 above my signature and wrote EXEMPT in the proper place, it was all over. No more expectation of voluntary taxes going to the IRS or State. Three years have passed, and not a single letter from the IRS, FTB or other Penumbra tax engraft. All the failures to file income taxes that agency sought were abated as each year was signed off, without prejudice, on the face of the presentment instrument. Twenty-five years of fighting facts came down to two words in Law; "Without Prejudice," and Maritime jurisdiction has no claim to action. No expectation of payment and the required promise is vitiated, because political issues are settled at law, and without conflict, my Personam Rights are reserved.

Black's. Tangible personal property is term commonly used in statutes, which provide for taxation of personal property. Your signature is property also, and you may use it to protect yourself and your property. Only the "entitled state Citizen" is guaranteed the Bill of Rights by signature. Statutes have no police power to tax a non-corporate citizen and must "provide" regulatory activity by "unconditional" devise, which is executed by Maritime jurisdiction and MPs for police power. Agency "offers" the same forum contract for the children in the schoolyard as it does for a ferret in your jewelry. If you signed something while in an ignorant State and waived in personam jurisdiction at Rule 12(b), revoke signature as soon as possible.

Article I Section (3) Representatives and direct Taxes shall be apportioned.

An agent would be very foolish to raise a constitutional issue such as this by violating your Rights and others by executing a "conditioned" instrument per UCC 3-104.2. This Constitutional section will now apply since we have represented our demand for "entitlement" per UCC 1-103:6; the code must be read in harmony with the Common Law, and relief must be given or Rights of Personam will be violated. There are many statutes and Executive devise which may issue presumptive delict to enforce implied power of agency Maritime jurisdiction. Selective Draft, Social Security and IRS are engrafts of Article I who created them and Executive "forum" of Article II replete with police power to enforce implied obligation. The Separation of Powers is only Law if We Thee People, individually, pray to Article III Grace.

A ferret has no chance before this Penumbra power, but alas, "Without Prejudice UCC 1-207" as answer to the trapper is from Thee Article III Judiciary, and except the shedding, I am good with my ferret.

Black's. Tax. Essential characteristic of a tax are that it is not a voluntary payment or donation, but an enforced contribution, exacted pursuant to legislative authority. Michigan Employment Sec. Commission v. Patt, 4 Mich.App. 228, 144 N.W.2d. 663, 665.

An enforced contribution using police power is manifest by the unconditional signing of subject matter forms to the detriment of your personam. We all work for a living and sign the instruments of our employers, which have "made liable" its employees by the implied legislative authority of taxation. The enforced contribution becomes "declared" unconscionable and void when the signing contains a condition, which is arbitrary to UCC 3-104.2 "unconditional." Without prejudice UCC 1-207, written above your signature, vitiates the W-4 at perjury and the agent who dares an "executor action," is personally responsible at the Common Law. All who touch the "dead in law" instrument become infected with the virus of Truth and all will be held accountable, for your conditional instrument cannot be changed or altered per charter of the institution. The income tax is voluntary; the tax on alcohol is not voluntary and is strictly enforced.

Black's. Administrative Procedure Act. Such act authorizes actions against federal officers by "any person suffering legal wrong because of agency action, or adversely affected or aggrieved by agency action within the meaning of a relevant statute." 5 U.S.C.A. 702.

"Agency action 'within' the meaning of a relevant statute," as far as punishment of agent, would be tantamount to a bite from a very angry ferret. Agent action "without" assent of a state Citizen at reservation of rights, has no power and "color of Law" 42 U.S. C. A. 1983 his yoke.

When Admiralty is Masted in your presents, beware your silk purse lest your pearls be "prize" and thing in action.

Black's. Magistrate. The term in its generic since refers to a person clothed with power as a public civil officer, or a public civil officer invested with executive or judicial power.

Generic is always a duplicate of the real thing. In personam is a copy of Personam. Human law of public policy attempts to duplicate Mankind's Public Law of God, and chaos is babbling at the Wall of We Thee People with 14th Amendment police power. A generic judge clothed with implied power may worry the ferret, but its property owner is "represented" with Article III.

California Government Code 22.2 "The common Law of England, so far as it is not repugnant to or inconsistent with the Constitution of the United States, or the Constitution or the laws of this state, is the rule of decision in all the courts of this state."

Obligating agency to this section of Law "within" a state is getting very serious as more of We Thee People use the Common Law found within the U.C. CODE 1-103.6. The Common Law of England originated with the Magna Carta of 1215. The Instrument is based on comprehensive principles of property, morality, justice, reason, conscience, Truth, and common sense. Basically, if you do not harm the state rights or property of others, and keep contracts you signed willingly, intentionally and voluntarily, the Law would protect you and your property. Unconscionable contracts of commercial venture are void under UCC 2-302.

The Natural born citizen is guaranteed a Republican government of the people; a government by representatives chosen by the people. In re Duncan, 139 U.S. 449, 11 S.Ct. 573, 35 L.Ed. 219.

Artificial citizens must accept what they are given by Democratic "public policy." A state Citizen is guaranteed a Constitutional republican government and "public Law" is in place if We Thee People declare our want of it. Article III Judicial will respond to government activity attempting to usurp your inherent entitlement rights, but you must declare. Voting Rights of the state Citizen have been "amended," into voting rights for U.S. Citizens of Congressional public policy.

Black's. Representation, estoppel by. It differs from estoppel by record, deed, or contract, in that it is not based on agreement of parties or finding of fact which may not be disputed, and is not mutual, but applies to only one party. Carter v. Curlew Creamery Co., 16 Wash.2d,476, 134 P.2d 66, 73. It is the effect of voluntary conduct of a party whereby he is absolutely precluded from asserting rights which might perhaps have otherwise existed. Strand v. State. 16 Wash.2d 107, 132 P.2d 1011, 1015.

Your rights exist ONLY if you declare your entitlement to them as representative of your personam signature. Agency must assert their rights to the "condition" in a timely manner or lose the issue by estoppel. Representation by lawyer also binds "persons" to Maritime jurisdiction and you waive Rights.

Detriment or injury or prejudice to party claiming estoppel, Abbott v. Bean, 295 Mass. 268, 3 N.E.2d 762, 768. Express or implied representation.

Without prejudice is an express representation of agency estoppel. Agency may pretend they did not notice the reservation and attempt to "engage" you further per presentment. Pardon agency ignorance and reserve rights upon the unit and mail it back. You are "not knowledgeable in the Law" and neither are you expected to be, merely be vigilant and pray to the proper Power.

Black's. Representation. Any conduct capable of being turned into a statement of fact. Scandrett v. Greenhouse, 244 Wis. 108, 11 N.W.2d 510, 512.

Without Prejudice, is a statement of fact at Law and cannot be prevented or ignored by agency. Lawyers could speak for you, but you must shake hands at the Maritime flag.

Black's. Prevent. To hinder, frustrate, prohibit, impede, or preclude; to obstruct; to intercept. Orme v. Atlas Gas and Oil Co., 217 Minn. 27, 13 N.W.2d 757, 761. To stop or intercept the approach, access, or performance of a thing.

An attempt to threaten or intimidate your "entitlement" representation is actionable. The state citizen may "estop" government activity when we bar, impede, prevent and preclude their cause by the reserving of all our rights "approach," which eliminates "access" to Personam.

Black's. Estoppel in pais. The doctrine by which a person may be precluded by his act or conduct, or silence when it is his duty to speak, from asserting a right which he otherwise would have had. Mitchell v. McIntee, 15 Or.App. 85, 514 P.2d 1357, 1359.

Agency is "in want" of jurisdiction to proceed and must abate. To remain politically responsible you must answer agency each time you receive presentment or as time goes, dishonor of Maritime instrument may bring action in personam.

UCC 1-207:9 Failure to make reservation. When a waivable right or claim is involved, the failure to make a reservation thereof causes a loss of the right and bars its assertion at a later date…

If you do not claim your citizenship entitlement, you waive it. Agency has jurisdiction to proceed in personam until you estop their cause of action with a revocation, reservation of rights, or rebut agent presumption of obligation.

UCC 1-103:6 Common Law. The Code is complimentary to the common Law which remains in force except where displaced by the code…

If you are an artificial person or sovereign citizen and have a negotiable contract, the codes will force agency to follow the rules of charter, but may not estop the issue. An entitled state Citizen has agency against the wall. W-4 is "dead in Law" because a condition exists upon the now non-negotiable unit. A "satisfaction and accord" is now present on the instrument as estoppel and the reservation of rights cannot be displaced by the code.

Black's. Equity. Justice administered according to fairness as contrasted with the strictly formulated rules of common law. The term "equity" denotes the spirit and habit of fairness, justness, and right dealing which would regulate the intercourse of men with men. Gilles v. Department of Human Resources Development, 11 Cal.3d 313, 113 Cal.Rptr. 374, 380, 521 P.2d 110. Equity is a body of jurisprudence, or field of jurisdiction, differing in its origin, theory, and methods from the common law; though procedurally, in the federal courts and most state courts, equitable and legal rights and remedies are administered in the same court.

A state citizen is born under the Article III flag of a Judicial God. Article I devise of Social Security at state Citizen Birth engrafts police power of Article II Maritime jurisdiction. IRS has raised its flag over the Citizen via W-4. Social Security was not contemplated in the Constitution but the IRS was. "Congress shall have the power to lay and collect taxes." IRS is Legislative and agency activity within the Penumbra Separation of Powers grows fat as We Thee People watch our Flag being raided by our individual ignorance. Article II Admiralty furnishes the IRS with police power of collection. Each Citizen must stand in Propria Persona or Article III will not hear you.

Equity is an implied power of very presumptive nature and must have contractual nexus to the subject matter for the most important part of a Maritime jurisdictional challenge, Personam. Fairness does not equal "probable cause" for the state Citizen But, if you do not reserve your Rights; you are not "entitled."

Black's. Equity acts in personam. Bouvier's Dictionary of Law (1856): Courts of equity have concurrent jurisdiction in matters of account with courts of law, and sometimes-exclusive jurisdiction. In those states where they have courts of chancery, this action is nearly superseded by the better remedy which is given by a bill in equity, by which the complainant can elicit a discovery of the acts from the defendant under his oath, instead of relying merely on the evidence he may be able to produce. 9 John. R. 470; 1 Paige, R. 41; 2 Caines' Cas. Err. 38, 62; 1 J. J. Marsh. R. 82; Cooke, R. 420; 1 Yerg. R. 360; 2 John. Ch. R. 424; 10 John. R. 587; 2 Rand. R. 449; 1 Hen. & M9; 2 M'Cord's Ch. R. 469; 2 Leigh's R. 6. 8.

A summons to attend IRS, insurance claims, jury duty, federal court, selective service or surrender a ferret are matters of account and the vigilant state Citizen may avoid these Penumbra by reservation of rights upon the instrument of action.

Black's. Equity Jurisdiction. A system of jurisprudence collateral to, and in some respects independent of, "law"; the object of which is to render the administration of justice more complete, by affording relief where the court of law are incompetent to give it, or to give it with effect, or by exercising certain branches of jurisdiction independently of them.

Inferior Maritime courts of Article II may ONLY hear subject matter, facts related to state citizenship or personam are heard prior to trial. The Law court mentioned is competent because we have not exercised our entitlement rights and we are attached thereto by unconditional obligation. The court of equity is not competent to hear a state Citizen Propria Persona.

Black's. In Personam. Against the person, involving his personal rights and based on jurisdiction of his person, as distinguished from a judgment against property (i.e. in rem). Type of jurisdiction or power which a court may acquire over the defendant himself in contrast to jurisdiction over his property.

For a sovereign citizen to be before an Article II court, waiver of "entitlements" by "tacit" or contract are required. Personam rights are easily "captured" by devise of equity. Your Article III flag is soiled from the scraps of an "inferior" masters table and each Personam of We Thee People must pray knowledge or the very well watched walls of our posterity will fall to the "golden" flag of Admiralty. Each Personam "forehead," through "social engineering," signs contracts of obvious grief without knowledge of Thee Article III Flag, and brings prayer of fear, yet your right hand is yoked to the flesh; assent to seduction is complete. Personam is Spirit, attach nothing thereto without knowledge or "court may acquire jurisdiction." If you are in doubt, Reserve Rights, and thereby no fear of the master refusing a scrap, there will be none, for you have "Captured Flag."

Black's. Liberty. Freedom; exemption from extraneous control. Freedom from all restraints except such as are justly imposed by law. The power of the will to follow the dictates of its unrestricted choice, and to direct the external acts of the individual without restraint, coercion, or control from other persons. See Booth v. Illinois, 184 U.S. 425, 22 S.Ct. 425, 46 L.Ed. 623; Munn v. Illinois, 94 U.S. 113, 24 L.Ed. 77.

"Justly imposed by law" of God emanates from Article III, as "probable cause" of crime against thy exempt "neighbor." "Other persons" are agency that controls the subject matter and you're in personam at Rule 12(b). Those who sign unconditional negotiable instrument and "benefit" from Penumbra police power "protection" are not exempt, nor at liberty.

Freedom in enjoyment and use of all of one's powers, faculties and property. Grosgean v. American Press Co., 297 U.S. 233, 56 S.Ct 444, 44680 L.Ed. 660.

Personam is your Choice of power to control every thing you have knowledge of, all else reserved as scraps. The "liberties" mentioned are waived by most citizens, through social engineering, tacit, silence or omission and obedience to the Maritime jurisdictional devise which captures Personam. The only restraint lawfully obligating the state Citizen is "true bill" of probable cause from a Grand Jury. You cannot enjoy a caged ferret; they need room to be nuisance and mine play in the front yard. My fence will keep the little guy within and my "entitlements, privileges, and immunities" will keep trapper without.

Black's. "The word "liberty" as used in the state and federal constitutions mean, in a negative sense, it involves the idea of freedom secured by the imposition of restraint, and it is in this positive sense that the state, in the exercise of its police powers, promotes the freedom of all by the imposition upon particular persons of restraints which are deemed necessary for the general welfare. Fitzsimmons v. New York State Athletic Commission, Sup., 146 N.Y.S. 117, 121. An imposition of restraint is not freedom.

State Citizenship is being waived by most and enjoyed by only a few. The corporate citizen must take what civil liberties are offered, "all else is reserved" for those who are "suitors" entitled to Thee Bill of Rights. Agency cannot impose restraints on all to subjugate a few. "Particular persons" are residents of the 14th Amendment within your State and are contracted, sworn, and subject to domestic product restrictions. The state Citizen may declare entitlement of Liberty and not yoke of "imposition of restraint." Political contracting to Penumbra engrafts from the "four corners" or "intention of parties" is negotiable. "Unconditional" units are your restraints; reserve your rights!

Black's. Term "Liberty" as used in Constitution means more than freedom of action, freedom to own, control, and use property, freedom to pursue any lawful trade, business or calling, and freedom to make all proper contracts in relation thereto. State v. Nuss, 79 S.D. 522, 114 N.W.2d 633, 635.

You must contract on your own and the only "proper" W-4 is a "dead in law" non-negotiable W-4. Think about what could happen, will happen and ensure your Personam, reserve Rights for Maritime jurisdiction eventuality.

The "liberty" safeguarded by Fourteenth Amendment is liberty in a social organization which requires the protection of law against the evils which menace the health, safety, morals, and welfare of the people. West Coast Hotel Co. v. Parrish, 300 US. 379, 57 S.Ct. 578, 581, 582, 81 L.Ed. 703.

14th Amendment "liberty" is "social organization" contracted by "public policy" Penumbra engrafts of Article I and Executive Maritime jurisdiction of Article II and restricts subject citizens for the welfare agency. The Fourteenth Amendment is an inferior court system for artificial persons only and do not confer proper judicial for a state Citizen of Article III. You must rebut the presumption of waived personam rights by contract or refute the error of the waiver at U.S. Citizenship. When Personam is brought forth, the court will have no "implied power" to proceed per Rule 12(b) and police power is abated.

"The states are separate sovereigns with respect to the federal government…" Heath v. Ala. 474 U.S. 187.

This will not last long if the Citizen within does not qualify his entitlement, and reserve Rights to be without the Maritime jurisdictional flag in their state court. The fed is quick with their erasure of state lines, Thee People are waiving border crossing of jurisdiction and domestication by "cruisers" of foreign Mast.

"All legislation is prima facie territorial." American Banana Co. v. US Fruit, 213, U.S. 347 at 357, 358.

A W-4 carries the flag of Congressional Admiralty, as does Department of Justice, Treasury, Transportation, Commerce, Education, Labor, Agriculture, libraries, hospitals, post offices, ferrets and many other Territorial Districts of Penumbra. "Prima facie territorial" is on the face of the W-4 you may be "required" by employer to sign and the unit has clear markings; Department of Treasury IRS. A reservation of Rights raises your state flag against such intrusion and declares the W-4 instrument non-assumpsit.

"Special provision is made in the Constitution for the cession of jurisdiction from the states over places where the federal government shall establish forts or other military works. It is ONLY IN THESE Places, or territories of the United States, where it can exercise a general jurisdiction. 10 Pet., at 737. (Emphasis added).

Apparently our schools, libraries and hospitals are "other needful buildings" of 1-8-17, because I do not see an actuating clause for Maritime jurisdiction and police power over state Citizens, unless by unconditional contract within Admiralty.

Article I Section 8 Cl. 17. To exercise Legislation in all Cases whatsoever, over such District (not exceeding ten Miles square) as may, by Cession of particular States, and the acceptance of Congress, become the Seat of the Government of the United States, and to exercise like Authority over all Places purchased by the Consent of the Legislature of the State in which the Same shall be for the Erection of Forts, Magazines, Arsenals, dockyards, and other needful buildings.

The U.S. Congress and each separate state may engraft the implied power of Departments between themselves at Article II, and subject artificial citizens ONLY, to their delict and police power. As enumerated within the jurisdiction of their Separate Power, Legislation brings all "artificial persons' to its obligation instruments who reside within its 'subject matter territory." Social engineers domesticate its in personam citizens to tax product, as it is intended per title 26. Only those who knowingly, willingly and intentionally contract their personam rights to another should enter these inferior forums of contract. A person from another country would be a "subject" of State jurisdiction at Article I. You must also reside within a territory or waive the right to state citizenship to become a "subject" federal U.S. Citizen. Tribunals obtain their jurisdiction by your assent and implied ignorance of jurisdictional fiat.

Black's. Ignorance. The want or absence of knowledge, unaware or uninformed, so far as they apply to the act, relation, duty, or matter under consideration. Ignorance of fact or facts constituting or relating to the subject matter in hand.

Personam of state Citizen is food for the dragon's flag at in personam, just say no. Article II courts have many agency facts 'within,' that I am ignorant of, so I stay 'without' their jurisdiction. The good news is none of them apply to the non-artificial Personam. Law applies to the state Citizen through Article III with enabling probable cause, and cannot be heard in Article II Courts without contractual assent. We The People have access to the simple Law of man, which are not intended to complicate our Heritage. With political knowledge we may avoid "government activity' in 'district courts,' 'within" our respective state. A few personal liberties exist within the Fourteenth Amendment by statute, as to generic the Bill of Rights. Those rights must be sued out civilly or legislated to their Territorial subjects by negotiable obligations.

Black's. Equitable right. Right cognizable within court of equity as contrasted with legal right enforced in court of law; though under practice in most states and in the federal courts there has been a merger procedurally between actions at law and equity. Fed.R. Civil P. 2.

The only way these two merge is per statute at UCC 1-207 "without prejudice," or the magistrate will be contempt to put your silk purse in jail for bringing up the Constitution in his Admiralty tribunal. Again, the state citizen cannot be a "merger" with any implied power without his permission or in tacit by contract.

Said the wolf to Thee Sheep, Why do you allow us to nip at your flanks? The sheep sayeth, your master has us yoked with his elliptical engraft and you bite if we attempt to protect ourselves or wiggle free! The pastured wolf sayeth; doest thou know the promise of your Master? I cannot advise my adversary how to be sheep among the wolf, for you feed us; you must seek competent counsel of your Master.

The Sheep may only pasture with the wolf, if the spirit is knowledgeable and as "wise as the serpent" who prepared the wolf. Jesus words to Paul of Sovereign Covenant have filled the Law with Truth and posterity for this Promised Land. Ask Luke 11:9.

UCC 1-103.6 Common law. The Code is "Complimentary" to the Common law which remains in force except where displaced by the code...' The Code cannot be read to preclude a Common Law action."

Do not even think that the Code will protect you from a common law action if you are "hiding," for the Law must seek you out within its proper jurisdiction. A valid contract signed unconditionally and voluntarily will stand as "satisfaction and accord," and the rules of charter will be recognized and negotiated at agency terms. If you are a "subject' citizen, you may be 'compelled' to accept the 'benefit" of any agency agreement put before you. The Common Law action will come within the "force" of Article III Judicial. Judicial will not hear matters, which have already been decided and enumerated in the Constitution. Some of those decided matters are property, taxes, travel, employment, private business, ferret, grand jury, warrants, searches, gun control, abortions, "smoking," seizures, or any other state citizen entitlement. The only time the state may be a party is if The People have summoned an issue of criminal intent toward property or another natural citizen of any type except corporate in the strict sense. Article II represents the State of California, Incorporated with federal forum statutes. The People may be mentioned, but Article III does not represent the Bill of Rights in Maritime jurisdiction. Inferior courts are Territorial and complimentary to 14th Amendment due process.

Your reservation to entitlement may be used as notification to a court of your intention NOT to appear in personam, for Now Comes the defendant, appearing specially and not generally "de bene esse." The "State of California' is 'vested' with 'implied powers" ONLY and "No change in ancient procedure can be made which disrupts those fundamental principals which protect the citizen in his private right and guards him against the arbitrary action of the government." Ex Parte Young, 209 US 123. (Emphasis added).

When we identify the nature of the charges, jurisdiction of the court, and the status of the accused, we can determine if we fall within the statute and the jurisdiction of the court. The State and the court are proceeding with "implied power" of Civil Law statutes and Maritime subject matter only jurisdiction. Subject matter jurisdiction is vested in the "inferior courts" of Article I Statutes and Article II Executive/Admiralty. The principles and modes of the common law police power are abated for want of probable cause and "criminal intent." See Davidson v. New Orleans, 96 U.S. 97; Dartmouth College Case, 4 Wheat 518.

When jurisdiction is not squarely challenged it is presumed to exist. Burks v. Lasker, 441 US 471. This includes supposed duties, liabilities, and sanctions—attached by way of statutes—for violations of said duties. U.S. v. Grimaud, 220 US 506. In this court there is no meaningful opportunity to challenge jurisdiction, as the Court merely proceeds summarily. However, once jurisdiction has been challenged in the courts, it becomes the responsibility of the Plaintiff to assert and prove jurisdiction. Hagans v. Lavine, 415 US 533, note 5. As mere good faith assertions of Power and authority (jurisdiction) have been abolished. Owens v. City of Independence, 100 S.Ct. 1398, 1980.

The state has two basic responsibilities. 1. An Article III court in behalf of Thee "People of the state" in common law actions of criminal intent, based upon probable cause or for victims of property damage. 2. "Persons" of corporate entity involved with domestic product, as foreign citizens, federal, State employees and corporations, of which are "subject' to their 'territorial" jurisdiction of commercial units and subject matter only proceedings. But, the U.S. Constitution binds the state in either capacity. Martin v. Hunter's Lesses, I Wheat 304.

Always challenge jurisdiction of Tribunal, if agency persists with action, there is certifiable fact of contract which has not been voided. If agency has expectation of obedience, it may fact you into a coma. Reserve your Rights!

As Plaintiff, the "State of California" is acting in its own interest and is the "person" allegedly complaining. The state is attempting to bring a personam action and is seeking a remedy for an alleged injury of non-existent rights, as rights only exist between moral beings. Bouvier's Law dictionary, 1914, p.2960.

The States own interests reside in its "persons" and negotiable Maritime instruments. The oath, under penalty of perjury on a W-4, is your promise to obligate and to "dishonor" brings police power and Admiralty is Masted to "action" for corporate Territorial State. Our political knowledge has failed We Thee People, we have waived our Rights, and enabled assent of our children to Penumbra.

NEGOTIABLE INSTRUMENTS

Black's. Indicia. Signs; indications. Circumstances which point to the existence of a given fact as probable, but not certain.

Signatures on W-4, banking, social security, 1040, summons, licensing, store bought ferrets and gun sales etc. This means they are going to demand that you either help them prove your guilt or yoke you with proving your innocence. When signed "without prejudice," the instrument is non-assumpsit, which means "I do not partake" of this unconditional and unconscionable obligation, then take names, and let God sort them out. The meek must be obedient to Thee God of Truth and if not "hiding," SILENCE and prayer, or suffer your flag being Masted. Honor all contracts you have signed knowingly, willingly, and intentionally; these are known in Common Law as "satisfaction and accord."

"The term (indicia) is much used in the civil law in a sense nearly or entirely synonymous with circumstantial evidence. It denotes facts which give rise to inferences, rather than inferences themselves."

The instrument you signed unconditionally has promises to pay a sum at a future date or license a Right in personam. Dishonor is actuated with your voluntary assent too agency police power. Live ferret possession, with reasoned cause, may get you arrested in California. A protected license or property requires "probable cause" for the trapper to follow and he hath not the power. A presumption is circumstantial, as is presentment, and if not rebutted the issues become fact and may be "summarily" certified by the tribunal and warrant may issue upon valid obligation.

Black's. Indicia of title. Generally, a document evidencing title to property, real or personal. Edwards v. Central Motor Co., 38 Tenn.App. 577, 277 S.W.2d 413, 416.

Your in personam signature comes to life as soon as an instrument is "dishonored" and executor will snatch your silk purse. We the People get a lot of mail to our "corporate persons." If we cannot prove we do not owe a presentment, we may with "tacit" dishonor it and be subjected to Article II Department of Justice through false teaching and implied power of Penumbra. The "expectation" or "promise" of payment has "made liable" your in personam. The negotiable law instrument is due and payable, unless "notice" "without dishonor" is prima facie affixed thereto. This answer to ferret hunters will save your property from destruction or contraband seizure. If you refuse to pay, or evade by failing to "answer," your Personam is at peril. We The People must turn and face agency threat, with UCC language of the "wolf." Answer every instrument as though it were negotiable. Rebut the presumption with "affirmative defense," certified mail as agent notice, OR the instrument is factually dishonored, and you have failed to perform per contract. Don't get me started on police power, by now you should know how agency obtains your in personam by devise. "Information" of agency must be refuted and "probable cause" proved or "color of Law" has raided your flag, again.

Black's. Indicum. In the civil law, a sign or mark. A species of proof, answering very nearly to the circumstantial evidence of the common law.

Signature is specie of proof. We must be careful what we sign into our political status, because agency facts are like a red light and siren; does not simply go away on its own. Circumstantial evidence becomes fact, which becomes "information," search warrants of vague 'confidential reliable informant,' 'person of interest," and gang sweeps of your school yard. Your sovereign flag may be taken in any action if authority of the MPs is not rebutted.

Black's. Indictable. "Subject" to be indicted. An offence, the nature of which is proper or necessary to be prosecuted by process of indictment. Indictable offences embrace common-law offences or statutory offences the punishment for which are infamous.

All federal citizenship status "persons' are 'subject' to process of any procedure the agency may 'presume." State citizenship guarantees the protection of the Bill of Rights. Amendment V states; "No person shall be held to answer for a capital, or otherwise infamous crime, unless on a presentment or indictment of a Grand Jury." Misdemeanors are contemplated in the Common Law. There must be an injury to a real person with criminal intent based upon probable cause. "No warrant shall issue, but upon probable cause, supported by Oath or affirmation" is the final say of Amendment IV. You must individually declare entitlement to your Rights or loose them to presumptive agency process.

Black's. Presentment. The production of a negotiable instrument to the drawee for his acceptance, or of a promissory note to the party liable, for payment of same. Presentment is a demand for acceptance or payment made upon the maker, acceptor, drawee or other payor by or on behalf of the holder. UCC 3-504(1).

The IRS considers your cooperation a condition of employment because your employer is a corporate partner. IF you do not sign the W-4 non-assumpsit, by reserving your rights prima facie, you are also a partner in want of benefit. The W-4 is of IRS issue and your signature accepts, through a meeting of the minds, an "offer' and 'makes' the instrument 'indicia of title." By promissory note and oath, you are now "made liable" by contract. Your employer deducts the "graduated income tax' and the 'activity" shows "jurisdiction on the administrative record." If you do not pay the correct amount or make an error the presentment comes. After all required warning and invitations to tax court have gone unanswered; dishonor, "Notice of Lien" and police power may rear its ugly head. Although the instrument is only notice, and not a "true bill,' the employer feels duty bound and exacts your 'obligation" from your pay. This procedure is executed with your assent to an unconditional contract and the police power your signature actuates. Many Patriots are in prison at this writing because agency keeps its jurisdictional delict hidden within the administrative record. The W-4 is the control unit on the record with your voluntary assent to Maritime jurisdiction.

Black's. Negotiable. Legally capable of being transferred by endorsement or delivery. Usually said of checks and notes and sometimes of stocks and bearer bond.

The executor transfers the unit to anyone who can squeeze the obligatory "thing" from you. The only way I have found to avoid presumptive instrument and "mail box policy" is to declare my "privilege" and force agency to prove the matter stated, otherwise you must prove you are not "made liable."

Black's. Commercial paper. Bills of exchange (i.e. drafts), promissory notes, bank-checks, and other negotiable instruments for the payment of money, which, by their form and on their face, purport to be such instruments. UCC Article 3 is the general law governing commercial paper.

"On their face purport to be" non-negotiable if "without prejudice" were on the face and which further declares notice of the unit's "dead in law" promise. The W-4 is a negotiable instrument at the "unconditional" signing, at UCC 3-104.1 and is a "must" requirement for its negotiability. A condition on the instrument vitiates "unit" obligation and the police powers are without activation. The contract will not sustain the promise at UCC 3-104.3, for the unit 'must' be "unconditional" at 3-104.2 to actuate perjury.

Black's. Negotiable document of title. A document is negotiable if by its terms the goods are to be delivered to "bearer," or to the order of a named party, or, where recognized in overseas trade, to a named person "or assigns."

Terms are settled IF, you reserve your Rights. "Or, where recognized in overseas trade" is Maritime jurisdiction. We Thee People must respect a commanded authority, but demanded loyalty is bruising at my heel.

This Truth stuff is much easier to understand and the best part is, God has given "understanding" of the words and I didn't make anything up, save the silk purse, sow's ear and the old dragon.

Black's. Negotiable words. Words and phrases which impart the character of negotiability to bills, notes, checks, etc., in which they are inserted; for instance, a direction to pay to A. "or order" or "bearer."

There are a few other words that matter for the instrument to be negotiable. MUST is real good but, UNCONDITIONAL is my personal favorite because the obvious happens; the CONDITION of "representation," of all your "entitled" rights may be written upon the face of the instrument, which makes the unit non negotiable "by its terms." The state citizen may amend any contract he perceives as unconscionable. Unconditional leaves nothing to bargain with, all is reserved for agency. The only good instrument is a "dead in law" non-negotiable commercial paper instrument. Drivers license, banking, real estate, 1040, social security, taxes, insurance etc., all have you registered as promising to pay sister Penumbra and follow rules of procedure in the event of dispute. The great news is; it comes down to whether the agency is able to negotiate the instrument you protected and declared entitlement upon as your condition of accepting license or W-4. The ones you do protect will give you knowledge and generalship of future issues with others, or if you choose, assent to the obligation and partake of any benefit you may, it is your choice, at least for now.

Black's. Negotiable instruments. To be negotiable within the meaning of UCC Article 3, an instrument must meet the requirements set out in Section 3-104: (1) it must be a writing signed by the maker or drawer; it must contain an (2) unconditional (3) promise (example: note) or order (example: check) (4) to pay a sum certain in money; (5) it must be payable on demand or at a definite time; (6) it must be payable to the bearer or to order; and (7) it must not contain any other promise, order, obligation, or power given by the maker or drawer except as authorized by Article 3.

For your W-4 to be a negotiable note, it "must' meet the above requirements or it is not a negotiable 'unit." When terms are met within any business sense, there is a meeting of the minds. Our political entity has decided that the contract is good or bad and we sign, most of the time, without a representation of rights to declare our Personam signature. The Code requires a contract to be on "unconditional" terms, which is unconscionable, for We the People have the right to "Obligate to Contract" or not. An artificial citizen per statute must sign unconditionally. Your promise to pay has been cast into stone after signing, or until you realize your ignorance and revoke promise by affidavit to in personam relief. The instrument "must not contain any other promise or power." The IRS will surely not enjoy your Common Law reservation of rights written across the W-4, but alas, they are helpless.

Neither are Common Law Trusts taxable, BUT you MUST know at least this material before you rely on any Common Law Trust. A foundation of knowledge must counsel or you may be measured for an "agency ankle bracelet." W-4 "must not contain any other promise" and must not be authorized when a "condition" of "without prejudice" is prima facie upon the instrument. Neither your employer, nor the agent may change any item, for the unit is worthless, and no action upon your personam may be certified.

"It has been held that one may buy his peace by compromising a claim which he knows is without right, Daily v. King, 70 Mich. 568, 44 N.W. 959, but the compromise of an illegal claim will not sustain a promise." Read v. Hitchings, 71 ME 590.

You may know the claim is unconscionable but feel obligated or threatened to sign. The instrument or "unit" cannot be used to authorize a criminal failure to appear and documents signed without prejudice are not admissible as evidence. If you do not wish to save yourself, please save your ferret! With the first indication of issue write "I hereby refute the validity of your unattested claim, without dishonor, I am not made liable," Without Prejudice UCC 1-207, prima facie upon the presentment unit. NOW your Rights will be violated if an ignorant ferret trapper takes your property, for that is "piracy' under 'color of law."

"It may, however, be settled that letters or omissions containing the expression in substance that they are to be 'without prejudice' will not be admitted in evidence… an arrangement stating the letter was 'without prejudice' was held to be inadmissible as evidence, not only will the letter bearing the words, 'without prejudice' but also the answer thereto, which was not so guarded was inadmissible…" Ferry v. Taylor, 33 Mo. 323; Durgin v. Somers, 117 Mass 55, Molyneaux v. Collier, 13 Ga, 406. "When correspondence had commenced "without prejudice" but afterwards those words were dropped, it was immaterial; 6 Ont. 719.

This is very powerful material for the Patriot in all of us. No harm may come to those who declare Rights entitled in the Constitution and enumerated by our Sovereign Father. These works cause a Truth virus to spread among agents, if one hair of your head is harmed, Title 18 and 1983's will issue to all who "action" with "color of Law."

Black's. Payable to bearer. A negotiable instrument is payable to bearer when by its terms it is payable to (a) bearer or the order of bearer; or (b) a specified person or bearer; or (c) "cash" or the order of "cash," or any other indication which does not purport to designate a specific payee. UCC 3-111.

Your W-4 is negotiable and in the hands of bearer. It becomes payable when the terms are met or from "the order of bearer," for non-payment or dishonor. Liens, summons, tickets etc., are of this type. Orders from bearer are easy to obtain with facts, presentments, appearances or not appearing at all. All the judge needs to see from plaintiff is if the instrument is negotiable and you did not pay it or make arrangements. Failure to appear becomes a criminal issue from a civil cause and off you go to ignorance and very poor generalship. The IRS does not go to court to issue orders. They have special treatment from their own Article II "implied power" court. The UCC protects Maritime jurisdiction and prompt payment is demanded from all who "promise' and thereby 'made liable" in personam. We Thee People must gain the knowledge God intended in order to make these very complicated instruments "dead in law" by having no standing therein. The instrument is payable if by "its terms" you sign unconditionally. We Thee People cannot be forced to sign an unconscionable document for there is no activation clause for slavery.

   Black's. Standing to be sued. Capacity of a person or sovereign to be a party defendant in an action. A state as sovereign has no capacity to be sued except in cases in which it has consented.

   The "State of California" is sovereign only to its "resident citizens" of the 14th Amendment, and State is protected at contract enforcement. A state Citizen may sue after they have notified activity agent of their representation of entitlement at "without prejudice." The state agent gives permission for a suit when your state rights have been violated, after your representation of "notice' or 'without prejudice."

   Black's. Standing to sue doctrine. The requirement of "standing" is satisfied if it can be said that the plaintiff has a legally protectable and tangible interest at stake in the litigation. Guidry v. Roberts, La.App., 331 So.2d 44, 50.

   Your unconditional W-4 is protected by contract and is tangible. The "Standing Master" of the court will give the collectors their next duty, which is seizure. If your W-4 represents your entitlement to Article III, a judge will never see it because he would not have jurisdiction.

   Black's. Standing is a jurisdictional issue which concerns power of federal courts to hear and decide cases and does not concern ultimate merits of substantive claims involved in the action. Weiner v. Bank of King of Prussia, D.C.Pa., 358 F.Supp. 684, 695.

   The "implied" power of federal courts takes them as far as the Constitution will allow. There is no amount of voting or petition by any Citizenship status or Congressional Act, which will amend a Bill of Rights. A Federal Executive officer or lawyer will sue a ferret, just to prove he has the power of obligating you to participate. He will then send you a presentment and force you to pay for the service. Reserving your Rights to property will change this scenario to squeaky toys all around. Enjoy your ferret; the little guys are as free as you are.

   Black's. Standing orders. Rules adopted by particular courts for governing practice before them. In some states, the presiding judge has authority to adopt standing orders for his court alone. They may include rules as to the time at which court commences each day, a procedure for requesting continuances of cases and a method by which cases are placed on the trial list of the particular court. They may be system wide or affect only a particular court in the system.

   This is beginning to feel more like, courts-martial. Adopt is the "engraft" of Penumbra. The "inferior" courts of most states have adopted the Federal Rules of Civil Procedure and engrafted Code of Military Justice, which has secured survival of Penumbra. Whatever they call it, the Masted Flag has captured our schoolyards and I really wish they would stay away from our ferrets.

Black's. Administrative Procedure Act. Such Act authorizes actions against federal officers by "any person suffering legal wrong because of agency action within the meaning of the relative statute." 5 U.S.C.A. 702.

Agency must follow "charter" and the UC Code or give you permission to sue the individual agent for violating your rights of contract for attempting to bring a "dead in law" issue back to life. You put the red light in their mirror for a change.

Black's. Standing Master. An officer of the court appointed on a regular basis to hear and determine matters within his jurisdiction for which a master may be appointed, as a master of chancery.

Chancery is a judge in the court of equity, fancy that, Maritime jurisdiction. Constitutional, without a doubt, BUT use of devise has captured our state flag and fraud will not stand in a Court of Law.

How did We Thee People come to this? My ferret knows the answer to this one; don't make me come over there.

Black's. Chancery. Equity; equitable jurisdiction; a court of equity the system of jurisprudence administered in courts of equity.

Article II "implied power' and 'inferior courts" of Statutory Procedure is Admiralty any way you spell it and We Thee People are empowered to remain "without" these jurisdictions by entitlement.

Black's. Officer de facto. As distinguished from an officer de jure; this is the designation of one who is in the actual possession and administration of the office, under some colorable or apparent authority although his title to the same, whether by election or appointment, is in reality invalid or at least formally questioned. Norton v. Shelby County, 118 U.S. 425, 6 S.Ct. 1121, 30 L.Ed. 178. "Officer de facto" includes one whose duties of office are exercised under color of election or appointment by or pursuant to public, unconstitutional law, before same is adjudicated to be such. Platte v. Dortch, 255 Ind. 157, 263 N.E.2d 266, 268.

Public law concerns the relations of states to each other and sovereign private individuals whom domicile within. "An Act of public law may be (1) general (applying to all persons within the jurisdiction of the act) (2) local (applying to geographical area), or (3) special (relating to an organization which is charged with a public interest)." No act, statue, or "emergency' can 'imply' a 'power' of jurisdiction upon a state Citizen after rights are reserved. If there were no difference in citizenship as it relates to jurisdiction, statute would not bring it up in the first place. The 14th Amendment is the Congressional playground of Article II engraft. "Persons' who reside contractually within the geographical area of Washington, District of Columbia are 'artificial persons' residing within your state borders and are under the jurisdiction of Article I and must rely on its 'implied powers" for remedy. The IRS is not special, nor is state Tax, motor vehicles tax and registration, banks, schools, post office, Commerce dept., FBI, DEA, ATB and ferret hunting Fish and Game of California variety. Insurance and banking are at the front of Statute subject matter Law. The wiggly tail of agency moves quickly upon those who are uninsured.

Black's. Public purpose. In the law of taxation, eminent domain, etc., this is a term of classification to distinguish the objects for which, according to settled usage, the government is to provide, from those which by the like usage, are left to private interest, inclination, or liberality.

If your classification is "person of U.S. Citizenship," or state Citizen, the government will take your voluntary W-4 obligation pledge as promised at UCC 3-104.3. You are being assessed for benefit or privilege at contract for presumed personal gain or benefit. Liberty to obligate is your Choice.

The 16th Amendment is the "implied power' to tax and 'protect' its 'artificial citizens' and the 14th Amendment 'implied police powers" of Penumbra government activity. Collection services at W-4 negotiable instrument is supplied by the "engraft" Article II, in the devise of police power, of which you assented, voluntarily. The specific individual and class are the "privileged" and "entitled" Preamble state Citizens. I will repeat! If there were no difference in Citizenship status, there would be no need to distinguish between "classes" of citizenship or jurisdiction.

Black's. Governmental agency. A subordinate creature of federal, state or local government created to carry out governmental function or to implement a statute or statutes.

Penumbra is the engrafted "creature created" to carry our captured flag to educate the people in "social engineering" Statute and domestic public policy. There are jurisdictional borders drawn to separate the Sovereign states from the D.C. Territory and agency does not have the power to remove the jurisdictional lines, at least not entirely, yet.

Black's. Governmental agents. Those performing services and duties of a public character for benefit of all citizens of community. The term includes firemen and policemen.

All Citizens include state and artificial citizens. Police power activation clause is different for each diverse status, reasonable cause for U.S. Citizens and probable cause for state.

These are federal statute words of art and hopefully you see through them. Hale v. Henkle states; "You owe nothing to the state for you get nothing there from." Maritime jurisdiction protects the forum of the Territorial State. We Thee People have no nexus to corporate agency, in personam notwithstanding. The corporate setting of today did not exist for our founding Fathers, nor was it contemplated in Thee Constitution of these united States. "Corporate America" lives off our own right hand with intent of our ignorant forehead.

Black's. Governmental duties. Those duties of a municipality that have reference to some part or element of the state's sovereignty granted it to be exercised for the benefit of the public, and all other duties are "proprietary."

The State only has sovereignty over "subjects," or those who waive their heritage under duress or ignorance at an unconditional "signing." Municipal interest are corporate and de facto without waiver of an "entitled" state Citizen. Proprietary are the local PGE, refuse collection, water, gas, and jail facility.

Black's. Private Property. As protected from being taken for public uses, is such property as belongs absolutely to an individual, and of which he has the exclusive right of disposition. Property of a specific, fixed and tangible nature, capable of being in possession and transmitted to another, such as houses, lands, and chattels.

An allodial title will protect your home by its presents on the land. A common law Trust, built on Personam knowledge will protect the rest. The State has "proprietary' rights over its 'District Territory' and 'subjects" only. We make ourselves subject by mortgage agreement and possession of "real estate," which are attached to Municipal "proprietary" units and "feudal" titles.

Black's. Proprietary functions. Functions which city, in its discretion, may perform when considered to be for best interests of citizens of city. Sarmiento v. City of Corpus Christy, Tex.Civ.App., 465 S.W.2d 813, 816, 819. Acts done by municipality for general betterment and improvement of such.

Municipal corporations acts on two distinct capacities: (1) governmental, legislative or public and (2) proprietary, commercial or quasi-private; the "governmental functions" of a municipal corporation are those functions exercised as arm of state, and for public good generally, whereas "proprietary functions" are those exercised for peculiar benefit and advantage of citizens of municipality. City of Pueblo v. Weed, Colo.App., 570 P.2d 15, 18.

Your local Department of Motor Vehicles, Waste Management, Child Protection, State and local police, fire protection, permits; license, schools, ferret hunters, roads and post offices are all a part of the corporate pie that We Thee People "made' our in personam 'liable" too. The states have adopted the rules and territorial entity of the federal government through presumption and "implied powers" of Article I based on "feudatory principalities, with inferior regalities and subordinate powers of legislation." 1 Blackstone Comm. 108.

The Penumbra beast has many heads, but all "must" assent to the negotiable instrument Code. Municipal devise must conform to the Common Law or the Entitled state Citizen may bring a "color of Law" action.

Chapter 3: Separation of Powers

Private Meeting; probably did not take place and the author is unknown. Edward Mandell House would have been a prophet to have foreknowledge of this end time. The writing to me is poetic in that it reveals many Truths in such a short time.

Edward Mandell House had this to say in a private meeting with Woodrow Wilson.

Very soon, every American will be required to register their biological property in a National system designed to keep track of the people and that will operate under the ancient system of pledging. By such methodology, we can compel people to submit to our agenda, which will affect our security as a chargeback for our fiat paper currency. Every American will be forced to register or suffer not being able to work and earn a living. They will be our chattel, and we will hold the security interest over them forever, by operation of the law merchant under the scheme of secured transactions. Americans, by unknowingly or unwittingly delivering the bills of lading to us will be rendered bankrupt and insolvent, forever to remain economic slaves through taxation, secured by their pledges. They will be stripped of their rights and given a commercial value designed to make us a profit and they will be none the wiser, for not one man in a million could ever figure our plans and, if by accident one or two would figure it out, we have in our arsenal plausible deniability. After all, this is the only logical way to fund government, by floating liens and debt to the registrants in the form of benefits and privileges. This will inevitably reap to us huge profits beyond our wildest expectations and leave every American a contributor to this fraud which we will call Social Insurance. Without realizing it, every American will insure us for any loss we may incur and in this manner; every American will unknowingly be our servant, however begrudgingly. The people will become helpless and without any hope for their redemption and, we will employ the high office of the President of our dummy corporation to foment this plot against America. Author unknown.

To me "plausible deniability" gave the whole thing away, but with Truth. This window is open through the use of devise contracts. Those who partake are "none the wiser" and voluntarily sign "unconditional" instruments, knowing them to be "unconscionable." "Clean Hands Doctrine" dictates, no rights have been violated if "satisfaction and accord" have been achieved.

71

The above would also prove that a conspiracy existed between men to deny the Liberties we have freely contracted. Equity today is the result of thousands of years of tested commercial devise to further enslave the Children of God.

Agency has no more power now than it did at the signing of the Constitution. False teaching is the adversary of the People. The 14th Amendment was an intentional intrusion upon the state Citizen.

For our failure to recognize others of the same birthright status, we have socialized ourselves into subjectivity. God is forgiving, but our test of Him will not be tolerated.

Like minds attract over this great American expanse and We the People need good Shepherds' and the scribe of Law or the double edged Sword of Thy Covenant will not weald.

Black's. Penumbra Doctrine. Implied powers of the federal government predicated on the Necessary and Proper Clause of the U.S.Const., Art. I Sec.8 (18), permits one implied power to be engrafted on another implied power. Kohl v. U.S., 91 U.S. 367, 23 L.Ed. 449.

The "implied powers" are Article I Legislative and Article II Executive/Admiralty. These "separate" powers are "inferior" to Article III judicial courts. Statute procedural laws apply only to artificial persons such as, corporations, municipalities and "persons" from other Nations who are visiting or naturalized as "subject resident" by taking an oath of allegiance to Article I Section 8 Clause 17 of the Constitution. Most of the contracts we sign "unconditionally," are issued as "units" by "sworn persons" who in turn "swear-in" and sign on We Thee People via obligatory instruments. These "employees" are personally responsible and liable if your agreement is amended or violated in any way after your rights are reserved.

Agents are put on "notice" when your rights are reserved "without prejudice" under Uniform Commercial Code (UCC) 1-207. The UCC is an excellent Law enforcement tool of Article III and Thee Bill of Rights. Agency must comply with LAW, when their "implied power" is demurrer by the Sovereign Citizen. Under UCC 1-103.6, the statute must be read in "harmony" with Thee Common Law and must be "complementary" to that instrument.

Article I Section I All legislative powers herein granted shall be vested in a Congress of the United States, which shall consist of a Senate and House of Representatives.

The powers "herein granted" must be "within" the language of the Constitution of 1776. The 14th Amendment of 1868 allowed artificial citizens and corporations to sue each other and attempted to duplicate some state Rights so we do not wiggle as much.

We have become subject, card-carrying corporations because of our poor political knowledge and we obligate ourselves to the jurisdiction of statutes and the police power at "reasonable cause." The sovereign Citizen is exempted from Statute law per the Constitution and the Negotiable Instrument Law as witnessed in the Bill of Rights and the UCC. If you reserve your rights as "entitled," you can call upon those rights to protect your signature from corporate agency "implied power."

We Thee People have waived our right to be free, because of our low political esteem, our contracting has "made liable" our individual in personam to be "within the jurisdiction" of the inferior courts, whose only sovereignty is over foreign residents, corporations and those of us who make covenant in ignorance.

We have forgotten God is our counsel, and Law our Truth. God will not withdraw from us; if, we use His Law. God is the greatest politician of every thing. We are given the ability and the directions to follow Law through His Word. The laws of greed and power have eroded our knowledge of the natural history of mans law. Penumbra has seduced the People with benefit of unknown beneficial limits and all we must do, to accept, is contract.

When we remain ignorant, and sign unconditional waivers to our rights, we invite Thee very worry of God and thereby punishment. We Thee People must never forget where our loyalty lies. The Wall We Thee People Stand is very Strong in Thee Rock of its perch. God is Law and Thee source of Law. My covenant is with Thee Father, if I must use the law of man, I will use it as Paul of Tarsus taught, and remind the adversary of my personal sovereignty to Jesus Christ and only to faith will I submit my right hand.

Thee reservation of Rights is notice to government activity, and will refresh their memory of what a Sovereign Citizen really is. I put God before me as though I have an army. My cup is filled with Thee Grace of God, and knowledge of Truth. I have a smile on my face that is begging to hurt from prosperous blessing. This treatise is to inform Thee People of Thee Truth and its benefits. Ignorance is the best place to start a good study. I will define a few of the words, but you will have to look up some of them. Do not read too fast, all the words are important and have hidden meaning within the corporate law "forum" instrument you sign and you must learn to "be as wise as the serpent."

Discovery is keen of Law and the meek will inherit the Truth found therein.

Black's. Forum contractus. The forum of the contract; the court of the place where a contract is made; the place where a contract is made, considered as a place of jurisdiction.

We are "made liable" at the signing of the "unit." The perjury declaration may as well be in Washington D.C. The W-4, Birth certificate, driver's license, bank account, or the myriad of "Penumbra" units we sign, influence our political knowledge of remedy, and directly affect our generalship of the inevitable infraction. The "writing" of UCC 3-104.I "must" be "unconditional" at UCC 3-104.2 to issue "promise" of UCC 3-104.3, which gives jurisdiction to agency and police power to enforce "dishonor."

William Dixon

Thee reservation of Rights puts a "condition" on the now, non-negotiable "unit," making remedy at generalship relieving, and at least makes us look like we know what we are doing. This will put the yoke on agency, they "must" prove their code is "complementary" to Thee Common Law per UCC 1-103.6 and "makes liable" agency to the burden of proof.

Black's. Legislative department. (Article I) That department of government whose appropriate function is the, making or enactment of laws. As enactment of law distinguished from the judicial department (Article III), which interprets and applies the laws, and the executive department (Article II), which carries them into execution and effect.

A "making" is of federal or State statutes from Article I and are the result of our government's involvement of commerce at corporate culture, social engineering and a very large helping hand from Article II Executive forum Admiralty via "public policy." Agency will educate your every step if you do not stick to the letter of the contract. Penumbra "government activity" has flourished since the taking of our "lawful money of the united States" and color of money has taken its place, but the Law of Money Stands.

Privacy acts require that all persons "made liable" are required to file a "return or a tax statement." What makes us liable? Penumbras "Maritime" nexus with your bank, Department of Motor Vehicles, Social Security, Birth Certificate, schools, vehicle registration, or other Penumbra contracts, has "made liable" your in personam to action. When we contract negotiable units unconditionally, though unconscionable, the Bills of Rights are waived. Our promise to perform becomes a negotiable "unit" at "dishonor" and an "implied" obligation in fact.

Black's. Obligation. That which a person is bound to do or forbear, any duty imposed by law, promise, relations of society, courtesy, kindness, etc. Helvering v. British-American Tobacco Co., C.C.A., 69, F.2d 528, 530. An obligation or debt may exist by reason of a judgment as well as an express contract, in either case there being a legal duty on the part of the one bound to comply with the promise. Schwartz v. California Claim Service, 52 Cal.App.2d 47, 125, 53 S.W.2d 15, 16. Liabilities created by contract or law (i.e. judgments). Rose v. W.B. Worthen Co., 186 Ark. 205, 53 S.W.2d 15, 16. As legal term word originally meant a sealed bond, but it now extends to any written promise to pay money or do a specific thing. Lee v. Kenan, C.C.A.Fla. 78 F.2d 425. The binding power of a vow, promise, oath, or contract, or of law, civil, political, or moral, independent of a promise; that which constitutes legal or moral duty.

The power of signing, unconditionally, an instrument of agency, results in enforcing the promise to do or not to do a thing through a police power of attorney, giving the corporation "implied" "public policy" mandate by your own hand. Without prejudice is a representation of Truth on the face an instrument and results in non-assumpsit, which cannot "sustain a promise" to "appear." "With reservation of all our rights," UCC 1-207: 3, under the constitution; UCC 1-103: 6, states, the statute must be read in "harmony" with the Common Law.

Black's. Non assumpsit. The general issue in the action of assumpsit; being a plea by which the defendant avers, "he did not undertake" or promise as alleged.

When We Thee People sign an agreement, and put a "valid reservation" "on the face of it," which is "prima facie," our rights at the common law are reserved. I am exempt on my W-4 and allow social security to be taken out at my discretion, per contract. Social Security will benefit some, and the most important thing is to protect whatever "benefit" you are due. Any contract with agency, signed with a "condition," vitiates the instrument. My bank contract is reserved as my individual personam rights dictate and other "implied powers," are "estoppel by contract" from "engraft" of Penumbra.

You can protect your children in their school, as well as yourself "with reservation of all our rights" per UCC 1-207.3. The social engineering of our educational system, has suppressed Thee Bill of Rights by having you waive your Rights at the UCC 3-104.1 "writing" at enrollment. Whereby, you assent to the trier of fact, and jurisdiction in personam. Rule 12[b], Federal Civil Judicial Procedure and Rules book.

Black's. Contract, estoppel by. "By contract," estoppel is intended to embrace all cases in which there is an actual or virtual undertaking to treat a fact as settled. It means party is bound by terms of own contract until set aside or annulled for fraud, accident, or mistake. United Fidelity Life Ins. Co. v. Fowler, Tex.Civ.App., 38 S.W.2d 128, 131.

Your UCC 3-104[2] "unconditional signing" has "made liable" your political UCC 3-104[3] "promise" and now your generalship must refute facts of which you have no knowledge. Presumed facts will stand, as good as an affidavit, if not estop with reservation.

Having an attorney is a waiver of your Sovereign Personam rights and binds you to contracted civil procedures and "subject matter" only jurisdiction. Corporations are not allowed to file affidavits to rebut the Sovereign redress, for the injured party must be in person or personam. The state cannot be a party unless there is an actual "crime" injury to a natural person with intent. Article III Judicial has the power to try individuals who have "criminal intent," but "persons" are tried under Article II Maritime jurisdiction. Statute criminal is "implied" power and is administered by "inferior courts," civil in nature, and applies to those who have waived their Rights unconditionally.

There are two sorts of "estoppel by contract," estoppel to deny truth of facts agreed on and settled by force of entering into contract, and estoppel arising from an act done under or in performance of contracts. Finch v. Smith, 177 Okl. 307, 58 P.2d 850, 851.

The signing of an instrument with your reservation protects your res, without it, you are subject to the jurisdiction of the Statute departmental code and the resulting procedural nightmares of Penumbra.

The settling of any dispute that arises, which is adverse to agency position, will put you on the receiving end of a presumptive strike at your personam character and tribute de facto, if you're in personam falls prey.

The individual sovereign is solely responsible for his own Salvation. We Thee People must have knowledge of the serpent, to be "as wise."

Black's. Estoppel in pais. The doctrine by which a person may be precluded by his act or conduct, or silence when it is his duty to speak, from asserting a right which he otherwise would have had. Mithcell v. McIntee, 15 Or.App. 85, 514 P.2d 1357, 1359.

This is also called an equitable estoppel and covers "false representation and concealment of facts." The silence works both ways, if agency does not refute the "conditional" signing, and allows you to believe your reservation is valid by not answering, you have estoppel of agency.

Black's. Res. By "res," according to modern civilians, is meant everything that may form an object of rights, in opposition to "persona," which is regarded as a subject of rights. While in its restricted sense it comprehends every object of rights except actions.

"Except action" to your personam, if you did not waive your rights. Your in personam will obligate your personam Covenant to the Master of Choice by your being sued. You become a unit of corporate agency when you do not reserve your Rights as a state citizen with "entitlement" to the Bill of Rights. Your personam jurisdiction is the right you give up by signing unconditionally at UCC 3-104 [2]. You are the subject of rights and must be a contracted "subject" citizen for the statute to apply. Lawsuits and agency activity must incorporate you individually, and "unconditionally" or loose "implied" action and police power stipulated within the now presumptive yet binding negotiable unit.

Black's. Civil actions are such as lie in behalf of persons to enforce their rights or obtain redress of wrongs in their relation to individuals. Fed.R.CivP.2.

We agree to the statute when we sign the agreement. A reservation is "notice" to agency, and the issue reverts to the rights you possessed prior to the signing of the unconscionable contract or obligation. There must be an injury to personam or property for Thee People of any state to summon an individual sovereign, who is not under contract to agency. All "persons" are those of corporate State who summon, and do not represent Thee People.

The 14th Amendment is where the corporate, artificial "persons" must apply for "due process." These are Article I courts of "implied" police power, with Article II Penumbra heads as judges who represent the Department of Justice and not Article III Judiciary. If you do your homework, you will learn to stay out of contractual reach of these Article I agencies and within the jurisdiction of Thee Article III Judicial.

Black's. Personal action. In civil law, an action in personam seeks to enforce an obligation imposed on the defendant by his contract or delict; that is, it is the contention that he is bound to transfer some dominion or to perform some service or to repair some loss.

A personal action cannot be had absent contract or waiver to your Bill of Rights. The unconditional signing is the controlling factor of our domestication.

Black's. Penal action are such as are brought, either by the state or by an individual under permission of a statue, to enforce a penalty imposed by law for the commission of a prohibited act.

Pay attention, it said "prohibited act," which can bring anything "reasonable" to action per statute of Article I. No mention of "crime" or intent. This allows corporate activity to sue a Citizen only if a viable contract and waiver to Article III court exists. The permission is the "presumptive" rule making of an "implied power," without your personam in mind and subject matter jurisdiction only, makes the good soldier, but leaves "public policy" to police our schoolyard.

Truth of the matter is a citizen of the state cannot be sued without prior notice and permission. A reservation is still a contract, but on your terms and subject only to your own personal ignorance of it, as to error. The burden of proof is reverted to the agency asserting jurisdiction. Do not "dishonor" agency "presentments" by filing them into the garbage, make agency prove their validity. Negotiability awaits the event of dishonor on your part.

We worry to extreme about what if, because we do not know what to do next. Each presumed debt and its negotiability goes into the administrative record the court will try.

"The law requires Proof of jurisdiction to appear on the record of the administrative agency and all administrative proceeding." Hagans v. Lavine, 415 U.S. 533.

Facts cannot be presented to hold agency claim as valid. The administrative record will show you have reserved your rights, even per statute.

We Thee People are Sovereign and our rights are written and inalienable within the Bill of Rights. The judge cannot issue edict without your "criminal intent" and agency cannot state a proper claim for "relief to be granted." I have been in this situation of court, and it is not the place for a Realist in Truth. Agency may persist at your stamina, but the proper affidavit as answer, puts them in a frame of vigilance and notice of your Sovereignty status at Thee Common Law.

A municipal bounty was issued for my driver's license because it is a "prize" in Admiralty. I have not paid bail because I want to be tried and found guilty first. Without criminal intent I cannot be tried, so agency plays the only game they can by offering commercial forum redress. They wait and see if you know that you can sue the individual agent demanding money after you asked for a copy of the debt instrument. The IRS operates the same way. You pay the "debt" first and when you loose they have guaranteed compliance.

Contract clauses with waivers, is the only way this happens. In this case it was for the lack of the public obligation to license. The summons was made "dead in law" by my signature and representation. I did not go to court. I posted my individual notice to the court via certified mail, which was an absurdity for a dead in Law instrument. I was notified by contracted municipal bounty hunters that I was in all sorts of trouble and had better pay up. My response was to build the record for the private collection agency so they would have to show the court that I have not "dishonored" their presentment. I wrote "without prejudice" UCC 1-207 on the face of the presentment so there would be no misunderstanding.

A controversy of over $20.00 requires a grand jury indictment, warrants and trial in an Article III court with a real judge hearing "law and fact" in front of the jury. My rights were reserved again on the next letter by answering; "I hereby refute the validity of your unattested presentment, Without Dishonor, I do not owe this money." I dated and signed the instrument, without prejudice UCC 1-207. I sent it back, certified mail to the person on the presentment that demanded payment. After a couple of years, the same letter advising me that they traced me through the motor vehicle files. The next letter I sent was a UCC 3-505, which demands the signatures of an agent under penalty of perjury, stating a verified and negotiable instrument exist. It is proclivity of your adversary not to answer and they did not. The IRS has also grown cold of me. There never was a warrant issued because the agency knew they had to have criminal intent to use police power; none exist and the required verification was unconscionable to the party-asserting claim. The judge would have to commit perjury to sign debt to me for my personam was protected and all rights were reserved. The judge did not have a contract signed by me to presume my participation in their agency activity. The facts and Law represented by my hand is on the record of the court.

The entire system would have to come to a standstill if the above were not Truth. The only other alternative is for the court to demand that you must sign an unconditional contract, the same as artificial persons and corporations. The facts, you agreed to, are within the reservation of Rights. WITHOUT PREJUDICE UCC 1-207, above your signature reserves whatever personam Rights you possess at time of the signing.

Agency "must" accept the "conditional" reservation of Rights or admit the "unit" is being fraudulently brought by Admiralty and your hand may be taken forcefully to signature. Man hath not the power. Artificial "persons," soldiers, attorneys, corporations, and ferret hunting fish and game "officers" can be restricted to an unconditional contract and oath.

A reservation is "prima facie" that "notice" is "explicit" UCC 1-207.3. Agency is estoppel and must not deny Truth as to the facts stated in your reservation. Agency is bound by the "conditional" "unit" which is "dead in law." Agency must accept your conditional signature or give up the secret they keep of your Law heritage.

Where there is no obligation, there is no right. Agency has only implied power, and presumption, which if not rebutted, "makes" an action to you're in personam. The permission or activation clause to use police power to enforce a "dishonored" negotiable and civil contract is of your own hand.

Black's. Presumptive evidence. Prima facie evidence or evidence which is not conclusive and admits of explanation or contradiction; evidence which must be received and treated as true and sufficient until and unless rebutted by other evidence, i.e., evidence which a statute says shall be presumptive of another fact unless rebutted.

This begins with the signing of an unconditional instrument that you now know to be unconscionable. We are presumptively giving our heritage of Thee Law to agency keeping and are realistically suffering the yoke of our own personal bad politics and ignorance of Thee Law of God.

When your "Natural born Citizen" state rights are waived, you may as well become a soldier and federal citizen. The intent of agency instrument is to "obligate" you in personam, so you may be actioned against.

We help agency domesticate our children via birth certificate, "education" and social security. When they grow up, perhaps another kind of factual presumption will yoke them, as the de facto selective service will do again. Government activity must contract and obligate, in order to subjugate Thee Rights of God's Sovereign People. We must be vigilant. A look at mankind's predatory doctrine will guide your Character to Thee Truth for God's very Spirit cries for it.

"The benefits of the Constitution are maintained only by a belligerent Claimant in person," Judge Learned Hand - 1947.

A mouth full of remedy, issued by Truth. We Thee People are witness to the most personal relationship known; Spiritual Law of Sovereignty with Thee Maker of It. Agency is estop from harming those of Knowledge in Thee Natural Law. A promise, that holds to this writing, for all of us.

The signature of our hand proclaims agency issues will be resolved by code procedure of Equity-Admiralty, which is certainly not Article III Judiciary. Insurance is not having knowledge of a coming event, yet presuming that it will occur. The bankers are heavy in this type of contract, as are States per "forum." Our domestication has resulted in civil disobedience as we search out the very essence of Life, Truth and Thee Law of it.

… "JUS BELLI. The law of war. The right of war; that which may be done without injustice with regard to the enemy. Gro. de Jure B. lib. 1, c. 1, §3." Black's Law Dictionary (4th ed., 1968), p. 995. "JUS BELLUM DICENDI. The right of proclaiming war." Black's Law Dictionary (4th ed., 1968), p. 995. Unalienable Rights "LAW OF GOD. 1. The Law as expressed in revealed religion especially in the Old and New prohibitive immoral, detrimental to the public welfare, subversive of good order, or otherwise contrary to the plan and purpose of civil regulations."

… "In order for decrees and regulations of a belligerent occupant of another country's territory to be recognized as valid, such decrees and regulations must not be of a political complexion, but must be in the interest of the welfare of inhabitants of area occupied." Aboitiz & Co. v. Price (1951), (4th ed. 1957 & 1968), p. 1317.

To be recognized as valid, a contract must be signed voluntarily and not forced as it is politically upon artificial persons.

"It is manifest, that the [federal] constitution has proceeded upon a theory of its own, and given or withheld powers according to the judgment of the American people, by whom it was adopted. We can only construe its powers, and cannot inquire into the policy or principles which induced the grant of them." Justice Story, Martin v. Counties, and so forth have only those powers granted them by statute, means the intention of discouraging conduct of a mischievous tendency. See L.R. 6 P.C. 134; 5 Barn. & Ald. 335; Pol.Cont. 235.

The Federal Constitutional right to "persons" is located at Article I Section 8 Clause 17 and the 14th Amendment. It is a very restrictive area and covers "subjects" within territories. Story was being kind to his master. The Supreme Court must honor contracts, is where he was going. A well-represented contract grows no room for entry of the silk purse or other mischievous tort. Article III cannot imply power on the Article I statute unless the controversy is prayed before them. Issues enumerated in the Constitution, are considered "settled," and no court in this Land may abridge or amend an Article III decision, but its situs may be challenged.

"Policy of the law. By this phrase is understood the disposition of the law to discountenance (dismissal) certain classes of acts, transactions, or agreements, or to refuse them its sanction, because it considers them the state. (public).

Law is not "public policy," and this is the area where our Rights have been taken away, such as school prayer, gun controls, and barter merchant, owning cash, ferrets and other property. All of Thee Bill of Rights are intact, We Thee People have not called upon our judicial power.

Confederacy, foedus (a public treaty, confirmed by the authority of the government; at Rome, by that of the Senate and the People): sponsio (between the chiefs of the hostile armies, without being ratified by the Senate and People of the belligerent parties; vid. Liv., 9, 5, in.: non foedere pax Caudina, sed per sponsionem facta est): to enter into a confederacy with any body, Hunter's Lessee (1816), 1 Wheat. Senate and the People): sponsio (between the chiefs of the hostile armies, without being ratified by the Senate and People of the belligerent parties; vid. Liv., 9, 5, in.403, 4 L.Ed. 97. "A Testaments. 2. Sometimes used as equivalent to the moral law, or natural law, as set forth in Christian theology." Radin, Law Dictionary (1955), p. 184.

Voting rights and representatives are more of Roman Civil Law than our Constitution, because of elliptical "words of art" that obscure voting Rights by Amendments to the instrument.

UNALIENABLE. Incapable of being transferred. "Things which are not in commerce, as, public roads, are in their nature unalienable. The natural rights of life and liberty are unalienable." Bouvier's Law Dictionary

(1914), p. 3350. UNALIENABLE. "The state of thing or right which cannot be sold." Bouvier's Law Dictionary (1859), Vol. II, p. 610. "[Unalienable rights] are enumerated rights that individuals, acting in their own behalf, cannot disregard or destroy." McCullough v. Brown, 19 S.E. 458, 480, 23 L.R.A. 410.

Your representation is acting on your own personal reading of the instrument as it pertains to your individual, political rights. You cannot harm yourself by protecting your character from predation. Simply stated, an individual who is born in a state has preamble rights. Mankind born in other nations are "artificial persons" by statute and are required to oath of Federal citizenship, "subject to the jurisdiction thereof," Article I Section 8 Clause 17 and the 14th Amendment.

Black's. "Abandonment is properly confined to incorporeal hereditaments, as legal rights once vested must be divested according to law, though equitable rights may be abandoned; Great Falls Co. v. Worster, 15 N.H. 412; see Cringan v. Nicolson's Ex'rs, 1 Hen. & M.(Va.) 429; and an abandonment combined with sufficiently long possession by another party destroys the right of the original owner; Gregg v. Blackmore, 10 Watts(Pa.) 192; [*6] Barker v. Salmon, 2 Metc.(Mass.) 32; Inhabitants of School Dist. No. 4 v. Benson, 31 Me. 381, 52 Am. Dec. 618. Fee simple title to real. 99 F.Supp. 602, 612-613.

POLICE REGULATIONS. Laws of a State or municipality, which have for their object the preservation and protection of public peace and good order [*management of civil affairs], and of the health, morals, and security of the people. Ex parte Bourgeois, 60 Miss. 663, 45 Am.Rep. 420; Sonora v. Curtin, 137 Cal. 583, 70 P. 674; Roanoke Gas Co. v. Roanoke, 88 Va. 810, 14 S.E. 665; Black's Law Dictionary (4th ed. 1957 & 1968), p. 1317. "Policy of a statute, or legislature. As applied to a penal or general proposition of local government law, subject to some qualification, holds that legislative bodies of cities, towns, villages, A general proposition of local government law, subject to some qualification, holds that legislative bodies of cities, towns, villages, counties, and so forth have only those powers granted them by the state (Bill of Rights)." California Code 22.2.

A belligerent could be a Christian Realist contracting his life away, being self taught to totally oppose any contract out of Fathers control. Dropping out was the only way to exercise any freedom and that became consuming. I sought "competent counsel" to protect myself. God answered the prayer and hooked me up to Truthful study material. Without knowledge and poor politics, I have gone down with the eagle, in flames, on several issues. I always walked away with a win. Smoking a little, but no sign of the eagle or remedy, more like a stand off; I won't, if you won't. My generalship has improved and despite all the smoke, the eagle has blinked. The eagle is with us in God's name and does protect us. I look at the eagle with more respect now for they appreciate your pointing out their confusion of your sovereignty status rather than compromising statute laws, which do not apply to state Citizens. The eagle will only recognize your rights on a personal basis.

Conditional contracting allows us to blend "as sheep among wolves" and protects our political Sovereignty with God as Thee Teacher. The barking dog usually has teeth, or it would not expose itself if it did not. It is not the size of the dog; it is the teeth that must be muzzled, with knowledge. My Master is Law, and I can follow to even extract the teeth if threatened or destroy the dog. Extractions are taking place as you read this treatise. The dogs of war will tell the eagle how difficult it is to eat what they are being fed. To save its dogs the eagle must give the knowledge of our deliverance, at least to the point of extraction. That is all We Thee People need to blend as sheep among wolves. We need our jobs, insurance and protection. We must not resort to weaponry or defamation toward the eagle. We now have the ability to have the Liberty God has Vested in this Promised Land. The Serpent is restless but silent and her proclivity, an assurance of peace.

Article I Section 10. [1] No state shall enter into any Treaty, Alliance, or Confederation; emit bills of credit; ON AMERICAN CITIZENSHIP BY JOHN S. WISE EDWARD THOMPSON COMPANY NORTHPORT, LONG ISLAND, N.Y. 1906. One of the cases, that the only limit of the State's right to exclude foreign corporations is where they are employed by the Federal government or are strictly engaged in interstate or foreign commerce.

The state may contract with those of its own "making" and instrument us to debt, only if we volunteer, even in "tacit," a signing or waiver. Agency State cannot force the hand of the state Citizen to sign a negotiable instrument unconditionally. Only contracted and sworn "employees" are subject to statute and "made liable." "Employees" work "within" the jurisdiction of our State, are beholden to pay for our comforts and are taxed because of their "resident status" as opposed to "domicile." The employee is "without" his territory of Article I Section 8 Clause 17. We Thee People are "domicile" (permanent) of our works and Liberty. The state has Thee number one job of protecting our contractual rights. The right to sign "with reservation of all our rights," UCC 1-207:3, allows our state sovereignty, and the right not to sign at all.

Black's. "Jus in personam. A right against a person; a right which gives its possessor a power to oblige another person to give or procure, to do or not to do." 1 Columbia L. R. 11; (1902) 2 Columbia L. R. 131.

This is our political weak link, in the chain of Sovereignty. The only right of State "implied power" is, an unprotected "obligatory" "promise" at "writing." Your protected Rights do not "oblige" the "possessor."

"But civil rights are to be distinguished from natural rights, which are such as appertain originally and essentially to man - such as are inherent in his nature, and which he enjoys as a man, independent of any act on his side." 14 C.J.S. Civil Rights §2, p. 1160, quoted in M.L.B. v. W.R.B., 457 S.W.2d 465, 466. See also 195 Cal.App.2d 503, 16 Cal.Rptr. 77, 91; Borden v. State, 11 Ark. 519, 527.

We Thee People are not subjects to "civil rights" of "artificial persons" enumerated in the 14th Amendment. "Inherent" "natural rights" are "independent" and "without" the jurisdiction of the State.

"Before attempting to answer these questions this court is of the opinion that some discussion is in order concerning what appears to be confused conception of the term `civil rights." The facts of this case seemingly are illustrative of this observation. As stated in 15 Am.Jur.2d 406: "Civil rights have been defined simply as such rights as the law [civil law-jus gentium] will enforce, or as all those rights which the law gives a person, a civil right is a legally enforceable claim of one person against another." Sowers v. Ohio Civil Rights Commission, 252 N.E.2d 463, 474. "Civil Rights are those rights which the municipal law [jus gentium] will enforce…" State v. Powers, 51 N.J.L. 432, 17 A. 969. "The law merchant, of which insurance law is a part, is said to be a part of international law, but is international only in the sense that the principles applicable are those that are recognized in all civilized nations. The positive rules of law themselves are but a part of the municipal law in the several countries in which they are enforced, and do not in any wise affect international relations; that is, the law merchant is a portion of the jus gentium.

Let us examine the former clause: "The Judicial power shall extend to all cases, in law and equity, arising under this Constitution." The case must be of "Judicial power;" it must be a case, "in law or equity," arising under the Constitution. The expression is not to all cases arising under the Constitution, treaties, and laws of the United States, but it is "to all cases in law and equity."

"Use is the law and rule of speech." By this law and this rule we must examine the language of the Constitution. "A judicial is one subject, a political power is another and a different subject. A case in law, or a case in equity is one subject, a political case is another and a different subject. Judicial cases in law and equity, arising under the regular exercise of Constitutional powers, by laws and treaties made by authority, are different from political questions of usurpation, surmounting the Constitution, and involving the high prerogatives, authorities and privileges of the Sovereign parties who made the Constitution.

"In judicial cases arising under a treaty, the Court may construe the treaty, and administer the remedy it has to; "The latter clause cannot touch the question in debate; for that only declares the supremacy of the Constitution [as it relates to the creation—not rights arising under it, to the parties who submit themselves to the jurisdiction of the Court in that case. But the Court must confine itself within the pale of judicial authority. It cannot rightfully exercise the political power of the Government, in declaring the treaty null because the one or the other party to the treaty has broken this or that article; and, … "The General Government, though supreme within its constitutional sphere, is yet limited in the objects of its jurisdiction, and in the extent of its authority."

So far as the Constitution has, either expressly or by necessary and unavoidable implication, conferred upon it exclusive powers, to that extent State rights and State authority are subordinate; but no farther than it can point out its authority in the Constitution does its jurisdiction extend over everything beyond, State legislation is supreme. In determining the boundaries of apparently conflicting powers between the States and the General Government, the proper question is, not so much what has been, in terms, reserved to the States, as what has been, expressly or by necessary implication, granted by the people to the National Government; for each State possesses all the powers of an independent and citizenship of the states, were not given the security of national protection by this class of the 14th Amendment." Twining v. New Jersey, supra, p. 94.

"The Supreme Court has relied on two major interpretive themes to give substantive content to guarantees of citizenship rights. Under the first theme, the Court has inferred individual guarantees from the structural necessities of the formation of a sovereign nation, except so far as they have been ceded away by the Constitution.

"In order, therefore, to maintain the position that a State has not the power to do a given act, which, without a transgression of international law, falls within the scope of the powers of any independent nation, it is necessary to show that such power has been transferred, by the Constitution, from the State to the Federal Government. These principles are so well settled and so universally recognized and admitted, that it is scarcely necessary to cite authorities in support or elucidation of them." People v. Naglee (1850) 1 Cal. 232, 234.

"To make us one nation as to foreign concerns and keep us distinct in domestic ones, gives the outline of the proper divisions between the general and the particular government." The remarks of Thomas Jefferson as expressed in a letter to James Madison (1786) regarding the theories of the federal government. "A State has the same undeniable and unlimited jurisdiction over all persons and things, within its territorial limits, as any foreign nation, where that jurisdiction is…

"This position is that the privileges and immunities clause [14th Amend.] protects all citizens against abridgment by states of rights of national citizenship as distinct from the fundamental or natural rights inherent in state citizenship." Madden v. Kentucky (1940), 309 U.S. 83, 84 L.Ed. 590, at 594.

"This part of the opinion, then, concludes with the holding that the rights relied upon in the case are those which belong to the citizens of the states as such and are under the sole care and protection of the state governments. The conclusion is preceded by the important declaration that the civil rights theretofore appertaining to national policy. Cases recognizing such rights suggest that certain individual activities rise to the level of a right of citizenship because they are an integral part of a function or power of the national government. Such rights therefore are not strictly "personal rights" derived from an entitlement inherent in an individual [traditionally vested rights], but are defined solely by the need to effectuate a structural power or function of the national government.

For example, in Crandall, the Court justified an individual's right to in [*1938] interstate travel on the grounds that infringement of this right would impair the ability of the [national] federal government to call citizens to its service at the national capital. [See, Crandall v. Nevada, 73 U.S.(6 Wall.) at 43; f. U.S. v. Guest, 383 U.S. 745, 758 (stating that the right to travel was "so elementary" that it "was conceived from the beginning."

There are many expected rights that We Thee People waive to the "implied powers" who "presumptively" govern us. We must be aware of their "entitlement" and protect ourselves with early representation, because Thee Bill of Rights is not automatic. Supreme Court cites which confirm our Individual Rights, stand at this writing. We Thee People must make our presence known or loose the Inherited Promised Land.

When an individual waives his rights to agency power of attorney is to "imply" jurisdiction, it affects all Sovereign Rights, because it puts us in a domesticated status and our Laws are designed, "in want" of duplicating the character of the Sovereign Individual and the source of rights. Truth is evident, for implied power cannot mirror character and spirit. I personally believe the government is doing the best it can to lead us in good faith, but with character and integrity being a natural mankind Law, even our government cannot reciprocate God's Civil Law to We Thee People.

Black's. Department. One of the territorial divisions of a country. Generally, a branch of governmental administration. Major territorial division of executive branch of government and headed by officer of cabinet rank; e.g. Department of State. Generally, a branch or division of governmental administration. Also a branch or division of a business. U.S. v. Elgin, J. & E. Ry. Co.

The Legislative contracts a Citizen signs "unconditionally" are of the "forum" status "artificial citizen." This is executive, and subjects you to the inferior courts of corporate venture. Executive Branch of Article II is not Judicial at Article III, and is an "inferior court" of Article I and Article II "engraft," represented as Admiralty and is "implied" law of the executive to departments "within" statute territory of Article 1-8-17. We Thee People are entitled to a Judicial Trial; with an impartial Judge, which is not of the executive. The jury must hear both Law and fact, as Preamble Citizens of our respective states are guaranteed a "Republican form of government."

Our government by Thee People has been adulterated by corporate greed and "implied power." State must contract its commands to its citizens of Sovereignty to domesticate them. Agency cannot demand, without command via contract, and we "waive" our Rights to Judicial review, because we volunteered for the program, "unconditionally."

Black's. Legislative districting. The apportionment or division of a legislative body into territorial districts.

Our mail system is a "feudal" zip zone system, which "engraft" the "implied power" jurisdictions and Federalization via 14th Amendment and domesticated "persons" "forum" corporate status. The presumption is that We Thee People will not recognize the yoke when we see it.

Your Congress and Legislatures are put into office to run the business of the state as a corporate State of which you are a presumed "resident" and corporate to the "forum" of the United States and "made liable" via contract. Their lack of sympathy for the individual citizen is apparent, for no character can be found within a corporation. The language is vague and obviously meant to be one sided. "Subject" and "artificial" citizens have no power that extends to your state Citizenship, unless by waiver, contract, "criminal intent" or a rebuttable presumption.

The so-called "victimless crime" is not considered criminal, because there is no victim or intent. The court "makes" a "failure to appear" a criminal matter to gain access to your "personam" status via de facto police power, and contracted "criminal contempt." You must give agency permission to judge your conduct, and "compliance" by waiver at contract or "tacit" admission to the jurisdiction of the Territory at Article I-8-17.

Black's. Legislative power. The lawmaking powers of a legislative body, whose functions include the power to make, alter, amend and repeal laws. In essence, the legislature has the power to make laws and such power is reposed exclusively in such body though it may delegate rule making and regulatory powers to departments in the executive branch. It may not, however, delegate its law making powers nor is the judicial branch permitted to obtrude into its legislative powers.

Admiralty. The enumerated powers of Congress are provided for in Article I of the U.S. Constitution. The legislature makes the law for those artificial citizens and corporations within the jurisdiction of Article I. The delegation and rule making are to implement the many forms and contracts We Thee People sign unconditionally to Article II. The executive branch "polices" our schools, roads, libraries, police, and other Penumbra. "Inferior courts" sue the citizen regardless of the rights we possess, for thou waived them.

A soldier becomes a G.I. ONLY after signing an unconditional contract. His personam has been given to ARTICLE II, Executive Branch and oath to the government of the United States. The soldier "must" "sign" an "unconditional" contract, "knowingly, willingly and intentionally," to fulfill the necessity being administered. The soldier has no personam rights or state rights and becomes the contracted matter stated as a corporate subject.

We waive our personam rights the same way. The soldier and the artificial citizen must swear to the contract by raising their hand, in a ceremony. In personam jurisdiction is not needed at trial because his citizenship has been dutifully waived to the armed services or federal citizen status. Violations that occur are judged by an "inferior court" "vested" within the jurisdiction of the "implied power" tribunal. Judicial is not allowed to interfere with these contracts made knowingly, willingly and intentionally by the people.

Article II Executive/Admiralty rears its Penumbra head when these two "implied powers" "engraft" together. The executive branch highway patrolman standing outside your window is there to enforce an executive summons. A summons demanding appearance before an executive judge under threat of arrest if you do not "promise" to appear in the Maritime tribunal by signature and oath is a voluntary action. You cannot make yourself liable unless you have agency license to operate as a commercial carrier for "benefit." When you show your license, registration and proof of insurance, the unconditional unit or drivers license becomes "prima facie," negotiable as commercial, via statute subject matter jurisdiction and assents police power.

The laws change willy-nilly, to suit public policy. Article III remains fixed upon its job of sorting out the Preamble state Citizenry who are vigilant of their enumerated Bill of Rights and Thee Laws of state do not, nor can they change.

Black's. Executive department. That branch of government charged with carrying out the laws enacted by the legislature. The President is the chief executive officer of the country and the governor is chief executive officer of a state. Used to describe that branch of government in contrast to the other two branches; i.e. legislative and judicial.

The Presidential power is restricted to Article I Section 8 Clause 17 of the Constitution, which defines the area "within" which both congress and the President have exclusive power, "without" 1-8-17 is de facto "implied power." The Union states are "without" the "implied powers" "jurisdiction" of the Legislative and Executive branch of the Federal government per the 10th Amendment and other enumerated powers.

Article I, Section 8 Clause 17. To exercise exclusive Legislation in all Cases whatsoever, over such District (not exceeding ten Miles square) as may, by Cession of particular States, and the Acceptance of Congress, become the Seat of the Government of the United States.

Government activity of agency cannot extend its police power past the subject citizen to the sovereignty of the states unless We Thee People invite the "benefit," individually. Union states are on sacred ground and borders which are crossed to compel Federal performance are closed, for the safety of the sovereign state Citizen. The state may contract with other states agency for the daily business of commerce, but the Citizen must be treated within the character of their individual status or the result is "ultra vires."

ARTICLE II

Section I. The executive Power shall be vested in a President of the United States of America.

Black's. Executive powers. Power to execute laws. The enumerated powers of the President are provided for in Article II of the U.S. Constitution. Executive powers of governors are provided for in state constitutions. The executive power vested in governors by state constitutions include the power to execute the laws, that is, to carry them into effect, as distinguished from the power to make the laws and the power to judge them. Tucker v. State, 218 Ind. 614, 35 N.E.2d 270, 291. California Government Code 22.2.

Powers of the state executive are defined and restricted to promulgating the proper laws to the various citizens within its jurisdiction and not to judge them. Did you ever stop to think of what Separations of power the judge was "residing" over. We Thee People are not subjects if we are not contracted.

87

William Dixon

This branch swears to oath the department heads and gives statute instruction to its forum "subjects" obligation in contract at bar. When We Thee People hear these forums being presented as mandatory, we presume they apply to all of Thee people, and we feel obligated to sign on. Executive cannot make the laws or judge them. The "inferior courts" are statute and judged by executive because their subjects are corporate and have no personam per contract.

This is the binding thread to our heritage, for it seems their job is to obscure our rights with "words of art" and to make us sworn personnel. An executive order is law for those subject to its jurisdiction. The "implied power," presumes we believe every word, and are playing on the same field as agency. In securing the due observance of law, the military flag has gone domestic in the courtroom, and subjugates our personam rights.

Article II Section 5 No person except a natural born Citizen, or a Citizen of the United States, at the time of the Adoption of this Constitution, shall be eligible to the office of president.

A Natural born Citizen is Preamble and born Sovereign in a union state under Article III. Free to exercise Liberty as he sees fit without license. Government Activity has attempted to duplicate our Sovereignty by obligating our parents to sign a birth instrument, which grants our birthright to the corporate State. A social security number is a negotiable "unit" and may be tracked and educated to whatever system of governmental civil law that is current. All corporate state citizen "persons," must then sign other subjective "forums," which domesticate us to federalism.

"An affirmative grant of jurisdiction is negative of all others." Burgoyne v. Board of Supervisors, 5 C. 9. "Consent will not confer [subject matter] jurisdiction." Feillet v. Engler, 8 C. 76. "Want of jurisdiction" refers to subject matter, not to person." Thurman v. Willingham, 18 Ga.App. 395, 89 S.E. 442. "The supreme court acquired its jurisdiction from the Constitution, and such jurisdiction can neither be enlarged nor abridged by the legislature." Ex parte Attorney General, 1 C. 85. "The Constitution has not clothed the supreme court with the same powers and jurisdiction as the court of king's bench in England." Ex parte Attorney General, 1 C. "The admiralty has jurisdiction over revenue matters." The Huntress, 12 Fed. Cas. 6,914. "Of the power of the state to authorize the license of all classes of trades and employments there is no doubt. But a legislative grant of power to a municipal corporation, to license business, etc., within its corporate limits, does not necessarily include a power to impose licenses for revenue purposes.

The distinction between the two powers is well recognized. Imposing licenses for regulating business, etc., is an exercise of the police power, while imposing them for revenue purposes is an exercise of the taxing power. (2 Dillon's Mun. Corp., sec. 768.) In re Guerrero (1886) 69 Cal. 88, 91. "Derivative. Coming from another; taken for something proceeding; secondary; that which has not its origin in itself, but owes its existence to something foregoing. Any thing obtained or deduced from another. State v. Wong Fong, 75 Mont. 81, 241 P. 1072." Black's Law Dictionary (4th Ed. 1957 & 1968), p. 530.

DERIVED. Received. Langstaff v. Lucas, D.C., 9 F.2d 691, 693. See, also, Connell v. Harper, 202 Ky. 406, 259 S.W. 1017, 1019." Black's Law Dictionary (4th Ed. 1957 & 1968), p. 530. "(Every taxpayer is a cestui qui trust having sufficient interest in the preventing abuse of the trust to be recognized in the field of this court's prerogative jurisdiction as a relator in proceedings to set sovereign authority in motion…" In Re Bolens (1912), 135 N.W. 164. "A suit by a shareholder [*taxpayer—cestui qui trust] to enforce a corporate [*UNITED STATES, STATE OF…] cause of action. The corporation [*UNITED STATES, STATE OF…] is a necessary party.

The government is not sovereign, without contract. The sovereign "implied power" is made obvious by the gold fringe that drapes our flag in schools, libraries, motor vehicle department, banks, insurance corp. and courts. The President is the contractor of that flag, which should serve as a warning that you are doing business with the executive in Admiralty Jurisdiction, disguised as Statute and considered Law by the innocent, but ignorant of Truth. All courts, other than Article III, have "implied" power and are "inferior." Only contracted subject citizens or the ignorant may be judged without probable cause in these tribunals.

The schools have taken the hardest hit. Through the years parents have signed instruments of enrollment, which ultimately gives the Executive "implied power" of attorney to executive Admiralty, which result is "police power" of federalized school Territorial Districts. We did not realize the subjectivity and domestication of it. The Admiralty flag gives no clue as to its intention. I always thought it was the pretty one. A gold fringe around the flag is intended to proclaim sovereignty over all who sign aboard.

We Thee People have the status of soldiers to the "Penumbra Doctrine." I will guarantee any individual a win, if they put a signature of Law before them as representative of all their rights and follow through with Knowledge and good generalship. "Without Prejudice" is meant as no prejudice can come to me for "I did not partake of it." These words are of ancient Law, and exist today in the Uniform Commercial Code and represents a statute approach to Thee "Law and Equity" of Article III Section 2 [1].

Congress makes the Law for its "subjects." Article. I Clause 8 Section 17 is all the "implied power" (Blks 5th Penumbra doctrine) the President has. Police powers are obvious when they presume to protect our children from being harmed by presumptive intrusions or for the sake of protection. The enrollment contract waives your Rights of Sovereignty over your children and personal freedom. The "presumption" is, you are going along with educationally domesticated "subject matter" jurisdiction. When we contract unconditionally, we assent power of attorney and "personam" is "subjugated" to "agency activity" and an inferior tribunal will manage our contracted rights.

We Thee People must not give up our sovereignty for another's contract. Our protection flag must put God, as Sovereign, before it or it will not waive. God has codified His Law into the Constitution and Thee Bill of Rights. It has been our lack of knowledge, and seduction to greed and power, that has kept us from Natural Law and Thee knowledge of it.

If the legislature has not provided a mode of exercising the jurisdiction conferred by the Constitution, a case may be brought up from an inferior court to the supreme court by writ of error." Ex parte Thistleton, 52 C. 220; Adams v. Town, 3 C. 247. "…a court cannot acquire jurisdiction to pronounce a personal judgment against one who has no residence within the state, except by actual notice upon him within the state, or by his voluntary appearance." Shipman's Common Law Pleading (1923), Benjamin J. Shipman, p. 23.

Resident is a "word of art" attributed to the IRS, which defines "employees" of the federal government, who are not eligible for state citizenship. They are artificial persons of corporate status, which are taxable and "subject" to the jurisdiction thereof" 1-8-17. We Thee People must have conditional residence or domicile. I do not reside in the "State of California," as it is foreign to a domicile and natural born Citizenship status in a republican state.

"Where the Courts of Law and Equity have concurrent jurisdiction, and a Court of Law has first acquired jurisdiction, and decided a case, a Court of Equity will not interfere to set aside the judgment, unless the party has been prevented, by some fraud or accident, from availing himself of the defense at law." Dutil v. Pacheco, 21 C. 438.

A citizen does not avail himself at Law if he waives his right thereto. Fraud is judged by its creator, and you can prove agency has taken your state flag by devise.

"Under our form of government, the legislature is not supreme. It is only one of the organs of that absolute sovereignty which resides in the whole body of the people; like other bodies of the government, it can only exercise such powers as have been delegated to it, and when it steps beyond that boundary, its acts… are utterly void." (implied) Billings v. Kall, 7 CA. 1. "No Law shall make."

"A United States District Court is purely a creature of legislative branch of government, generally provided for by Constitution, but not a constitutional court in stricter sense and its jurisdiction comes from Congress." Cochran v. St. Paul & Tacoma Lumber Co. (1947), 73 F.Supp. 288 & 291. [Therefore, the United States District Court is an agency of Congress.]

Article I Congressional "implied power" in Statute and the "inferior court" of the Executive Branch "makes liable" "subjects" only. The two "engrafted" Branches of Statute/Admiralty must contract with We Thee People or fail to have sovereignty over us.

I am a subject of God and there can be no other master. An agency functioning under the Law must respect the status of a free man and follow our Laws as they are written. I am hopeful that more of We Thee People will protect themselves with a reservation of their Constitutional Laws, enumerated in Thee Bill of Rights, and thereby bind the hands of agency mischief to his own contract.

The individual corporate agent will be the person who is educated first by the power of the Article III Sovereign Citizen. The signing, with

Rights reserved, is "notice" that I individually, do not partake of the system being promulgated. I have expressed the instrument to be "unconscionable" and abrogated.

If court is necessary, generalship will win with documentation of the "conditional" signing, of which the court is on notice, with copy. The court must act as Judicial and read the statute as "complementary" to Thee Common Law. The fact of the matter stated will not match the state corporate charter, and cannot "state a cause where relief can be granted." "Remedy" is dismissal at "limited liability," because there is no "intent" to obligate, at the signing, thus no promise appears "prima facie" on the instrument. Most "writing" at signature are under duress and induced by fraud. We Thee People have been seduced by presumptive benefit and protections of agency activity "devise."

Black's. Ultra vires act of municipality is one which is beyond powers conferred upon it by law. Charles v. Town of Jeanerette, Inc. La.App., 234 So.2d 794, 798.

Municipalities and corporations are "persons" of Article I Statute, and Article II forum inferior actions. The states have taken to the same forum of Legislative police "piracy" in their quest to "Executize" Admiralty jurisdiction within its State. Artificial Citizens share the same contracting Penumbra as the silent sovereignty.

When property is condemned, towed or forbidden, you can look at the 14th Amendment for the confusion and illusion of Thee Bill of Rights in its "due process" mirror. Those of us who pray for counsel and have chosen the less complicated path of defensive politics and worship the beast, have contributed to ignorance. Thought requires personal character, corporate has none, and does not translate well as it only lives to rule the character by mirroring "political culture" and applying "social engineering" to enforce procedure of "implied" "public policy." If all else fails you, think of implied as darkness in the mirror. A little knowledge will demand light from within any document. If fraud and unconscionability is present, don't do it, unless you reserve your common Law Rights within Thee Law given you by God's own hand. Thee Constitution of Thee united States of America guarantees each separate state, that Thee Law of Thee People, By Thee People shall not perish from this earth. Our Republican form of government, with Laws enumerated with the blessing of God, are guaranteed and inalienable.

ARTICLE III

"The Sovereignty of the state resides in the people thereof." California, Title I, Article I, 100.
"The Common Law of England, so far as it is not repugnant to or inconsistent with the Constitution of the United States, or the Constitution or the laws of this State, is the rule of decision in all the courts of this state." 22.2 Calif. Government Code.

The executive must assist the sovereign Citizen with Law and see that the constitution is adhered to when declared. The judicial power is the salvation of Thee Bill of Rights. The Supreme Court is the original Court of Jurisdiction for all state Citizens.

"Residence and Citizenship are wholly different things within the meaning of the Constitution and the laws defining and regulating the jurisdiction of the circuit courts of the United States; and a mere averment of residence in a particular State is not an averment of Citizenship in that state for the purposes of jurisdiction." Steigleder v. McQuesten, 198 U.S. 143.

"The jurisdiction of the courts as established by the Constitution cannot be altered by the legislature." Thompson v. Williams, 6 C. 88; Hicks v. Bell, 3 C. 219; Burgoyne v. Board of Supervisors, 5 C. 9. "Consent of the parties cannot give jurisdiction which constitution denies." Feillett v. Engler, 8 C. 76. "[Courts are to] declare the law, not to make it." Appeal of North Beach & M. R. Co. (1867), 32 C. 499, 529; Porter v. Brooks (1868), 35 C. 199, 210. "An affirmative grant of jurisdiction is negative of all others." Burgoyne v. Board of Supervisors, 5 C. 9. "Consent will not confer [subject matter] jurisdiction." Feillet v. Engler, 8 C. 76. "Want of jurisdiction" refers to subject matter, not to person." Thurman v. Willingham, 18 Ga.App. 395, 89.

"In the United States the people are sovereign and the government cannot sever its relationship to the people by taking away their citizenship. Afroyim v. Fusk, 387 US 253.

Citizenship status changes from state to federal citizenship at the signing of an agreement. When you sign with reservation of your rights, the agency has no choice but to accept your "condition," which will allow you to keep the Sovereign status and get the attention of Article III, Judicial. Study will give you knowledge, and any issue arising from your protected political, will pay dividends in blessing from our Father when your generalship is necessary. We Thee People must stand the wall together or agency will take our watch. When the State puts a contract before you, you must have knowledge of the issue or do not sign unconditionally. "Let no more be said about confidence in men, but bind them down from mischief with the chains of the Constitution!" Thomas Jefferson.

"Sovereignty itself is, of course, not subject to law for it is the author and source of law. Yick Wo v. Hopkins and Woo Lee v. Hopkins 118 US 356.

"The claim and exercise of a Constitutional Right cannot be converted into a crime." Miller v. U.S.

"The general rule is that an unconstitutional stature, though having the form and name of law, is in reality no law, but is wholly void and ineffective for any purpose; since its unconstitutionality dates from the time of its enactment. In legal contemplation, it is as inoperative as if it had never been passed. Since an unconstitutional law is void, the general principles follow that it imposes no duties, confers no rights, creates no office, bestows not power or authority on anyone, affords no protection and justifies no acts performed under it. Avoid act cannot be legally consistent with a valid one. An unconstitutional law cannot operate to supersede any existing valid law. Indeed, insofar as a statue runs counter to the fundamental law of the land, it is superseded thereby.

No one is bound to obey an unconstitutional law and no courts are bound to enforce it." 16 Am.Jur 2d. 177, late Am Jur 2d. 256.

The contract is the place to think about your natural political Rights. An unconditional signing is voluntary and subjugates the Citizen to the forum agency and "inferior courts." Citizenship status is altered to federal jurisdiction and no Bill of Rights or Article III court can interfere with the contract until it is amended by the "individual in person."

"Waivers of Constitutional rights not only must be voluntary, they must be knowingly intelligent acts done with sufficient awareness of the relevant circumstances and consequences." Brady v. U.S. 742 at 748.

The negotiable units of Penumbra doctrine are powerful in there knowledge of contracting and use of police power. Court procedure consist of a contracted Citizen under Article I jurisdiction by tacit or devise, Article II Executive attorney who represents the interest of the Article I State, and Article II inferior judge who cannot extend to judicial Article III because he cannot try an individual state Citizen with personam. Result is subject matter only jurisdiction and contract required to "tax" action upon the subject by using Maritime police power and confiscation activity.

A state court would be called by Thee People via a grand jury returning a true bill of probable cause to fetch the wrong doer with de jure police power because a crime has been committed. A warrant will issue and court convened. A jury of peers will hear facts and law. The People will be represented by the Article II Governor Executive to provide Common Law at Calif. Code 22.2. Article III Judge will hear testimony of witness and the Citizen is presumed innocent until proven guilty of violating a Law against God. This is the type of court we the People must find ourselves or worry will be our "prize."

"Included in the right of personal liberty and the right of private property - partaking of the nature of each is the right to make contracts for the acquisition of property. Chief among such contracts is that of personal employment, by which labor and other services are exchanged for money and other forms of property." Coppage v. Kansas, 232 U.S. .1, at 14.

The contract for my ferret was an easy task and protects her from the "contraband" law of police power. I simply reserved all of my Rights on the bill of sale. I must commit a "criminal intent" and the grand jury would need an indictment of my Persona to get at any property with my Sovereign signature attached "prima facie." The "notice" of ownership is in plain site, as my personal reservation of all rights.

"The term [liberty] …denotes not merely freedom from bodily restraint but also the right of the individual to contract, to engage in any of the common occupations of life, to acquire useful knowledge, to marry, to establish a home and bring up children, to worship God according to the dictates of this own conscience… The established doctrine is that this liberty may not be interfered with, under the guise of protecting public interest, by legislative action." Meyer v. Nebraska, 262 U.S. 390, 399, 400.

A Right cannot be reduced to privilege by statute. The Rights can and are waived by your own hand in obedience to the "unconditional" signing, which results in a promised obligation and police action. For example, the IRS is a creature of Article I "implied power," which is executed by the Executive branch of the federal government, which "makes" the issue Admiralty. All government sovereignty over the people is "implied." The federal implied powers are not after We Thee People for taxation. The "subjects," "under the jurisdiction thereof" are targeted. When we contract unconditionally, we waive our state Citizenship and become a Federal citizen by design, and join the mass as artificial in culture.

We Thee People have made ourselves subjects to the wrong master with our own hand. I wish not to give covenant to those portions of an obligation that I may find unconscionable, and which violate my rights with God and his Word within Thee Bill of Rights and Article III Judicial Power. I will not accept the unknown benefit, which has not been disclosed in full, prior to a signing.

"Government activity" contracts are unconscionable by the mere fact that a condition cannot be placed anywhere within it, for such would not allow total control over the issue not foreseen at the signing.

If it sounds like insurance, it most definitely is. I wish to avoid a bank account signing that will give the IRS access to my funds via the "engraft" Penumbra. A "notice of lien" is not a court order, yet employers, unemployment insurance, accountants, municipal police power, imminent domain, postal, schools, motor vehicles, and protection services will take your money, information, tow your vehicle, and take your ferret because they have your waiver or signature which has been turned into a "negotiable unit," which carries a full broadside of police power. Absolute "implied power" is still only implied, and remains "presumptive," and is easily "rebutted" "ab initio."

Black's. Confession and avoidance. A plea in confession and avoidance is one which avows and confesses the truth of the averments if fact in the complaint or declaration, either expressly or by implication, but the proceeds to allege new matter which tends to deprive the facts admitted of their ordinary legal effect, or to obviate, neutralize, or avoid them. Sievers v. Brown, 216 Miss. 801, 63 So.2d 217, 219.

Our reservation blesses us with the Judicial Power of entitlement to Sovereignty and rebuts an issue to avoid its liabilities or benefits according to their "Complimentary" or "Harmony" in interpretation at Common Law, Uniform Commercial Code 1-103:6. The UCC directs Remedy at 1-207 and We Thee People, who did not violate civil Law with criminal intent or harm any individual or property, may ask for Grace. My covenant is with God as Sovereign. I do not worry, and my political Spirit is draped with Thee Law of God's own making and I prosper in Reality of Thee Word in Truth in Jesus Christ. Statesmanship has been put to scribe as witness to those who are lost, and on the edge of signing Thee greatest Covenant of all time. Jesus Christ is Thee Reality of life, and Thee Law of Mankind has been codified into Thee Bill of Rights. Ignorance is no longer a consideration for the breaking of Covenant with your Personal Savior and intercedes.

Attorneys are "officers of the court," and cannot represent any "thing" other than an "artificial person" or contracting corporation. "Competent counsel" is impossible to obtain in the "public policy" court. Procedural civil law "inferior court" systems may only hear subject matter and use "color of law" to obligate personam.

The administrative record is where the Thee People must gain knowledge of Thee Law. We Thee People only need to know a few key words, and the Constitution will do the rest with vigilance. A very high percentage of most issues are resolved at the administrative level.

With a well placed political hit of "condition," at the heart of the "unconscionable" contracting unit will bring blessings of Liberty, because our personal covenant in Jesus Christ protects us with His Grace. Agency cannot produce a negotiable instrument, because the "unit" "must" be "unconditional" UCC 3-104(2) unless abrogated. Our reservation of Rights vitiates the agreement and "cannot sustain a promise" as UCC 3-104(3) requires. An issue of agency is "ultra vires" and a tort if pursued and each agent who attempts to duplicate or resurrect the now "dead in law" "thing in action" are "made liable" to the Citizen whose Rights have been "explicit," UCC 1-207:3.

Black's. Ultra vires. Acts beyond the scope of the powers of a corporation, as defined by its charter or laws of state of a corporation. State ex rel. v. Holston Trust Co., 168 Tenn. 546, 79 S.W.2d 1012, 1016.

Federal government activity has Congressional mandate to make laws, which effect commercial, artificial "persons," and citizens born within the territorial, jurisdictional and contractual boundaries of Washington D. C. and Territorial States such as Puerto Rico, ONLY. Government agency of your respective state has the same "implied power" over subject citizens. The state can only use the "inferior court" to sue out the contracts, We Thee People "unconditionally" sign when we seek "privilege and benefit."

Amendment X [1798] the powers not delegated to the United States by the Constitution, nor prohibited by it to the states, are reserved to the states respectively, or to the people.

If the implied power you face is not following the enumerated Bill of Rights and other liberties, you have a contract somewhere that needs to be abrogated, because state citizens are not "persons" "subject" to the federalized 14th Amendment. The state legislature cannot use the civil law to regulate, and domesticate the people by license and taxation; they can only contract "civil rights" and trick us into waiving the rest. We Thee People have the Right to contract per Article I Section 10 [1]; No state shall enter any Treaty, Alliance, or Confederation; pass any bill of attainder, ex post facto law, or Law impairing the Obligation of Contracts.

I think the state has violated every one of these and all done with the voluntarily aid of the citizen. Contracts are obligations, and government activity feeds itself with "constructive knowledge" of its "subjects."

Black's. Constructive contract. A species of contracts which arise, not from the intent of the parties, but from the operation of law to avoid an injustice. These are sometimes referred to as quasi contracts or contracts implied in law as contrasted with contracts implied in fact which are real contracts expressing the intent of the parties by conduct rather than by words. Power-Matics Inc. v. Ligotti, 79 N.J.Super. 294, 191 A.2d 483, 489.

Corporate "injustice" deserves the "implied" power of the "inferior courts," for they have chartered together as "engraft" agency, and contracted with the Penumbra statute "departments" empowered by the 14th Amendment due process. Anytime the implied word comes up, think rumor and presumption. When We Thee people start signing our contracts with our own personal reservation, we do not waive, but call upon the very power of Law.

Chapter 4: Thee Sovereign Exemption

My personal Sovereign and Savior is Jesus Christ. There is no other. The only direction I am to take is Covenant of Truth. The Bill of Rights at 1st Amendment and Thee Bible are my direction and standard for competent counsel.

A Sovereign Citizen cannot be punished for sincerely held religious convictions, U.S. v. Cheek.

Biblical Law at "Common Law" supersedes all laws, and "Christianity is custom, custom is Law." Robin v. Hardaway 1790.

God created man and has Sovereign Rights to our works. When man creates a "thing" it becomes property and distributed to other men in truthful dealings. Agency has "made liable" the people at contract with diverse weights and sustains promise with a "signing". The administrative record will show the "master" with whom we Covenant. This beguile is achieved by an unrevealed "benefit" and is unlawful to Covenant of God. Many have not read Thee Constitution of These united States. Do not take my word for this but, Thee New Covenant is witness to Thee Bill of Rights and Article III.

Churches marry the people to the State and pledge the congregation by filing a Corp. 501-c(3). The Bible is declared the true word of God in Public Law 97-280.

I do not see the benefit of two people marrying in the eyes of the State. State then covets control of our children, and "educates" them without knowledge of God. For what "benefit" to Thee sheep, when the wolf is stalking? Beguiled "artificial" "persons" must "create" other artificial persons or the Beast will die. Contracts We Thee People sign "unconditionally" every day are the administrative records way of telling us that we are not sovereign, the State is sovereign. Agency has far more of us sheep than they deserve. God is looking yet for His Creative Man to step forward with His Staff of Law.

Matthew 17:24, Jesus and the disciples were at Capernaum. The tax collectors came to Peter, and ask him if Jesus paid the tax. Peter spoke by design in saying, yes. Jesus asks Simon, if the King's children pay the tax or do strangers give tribute. Peter advised Jesus that strangers paid the tax, and Caesar's children did not. Jesus said, "so shall my children be free." In these united States, even Caesar's children pay the tax or use diverse to evade. Sovereign citizens, artificial citizens or foreigners are "made liable" for the tax via contract. Thee People do not require church exemption nor license to prosper.

Matthew 22:21, Jesus said "Give to Caesar what is Caesar's and to God what is God's." The Pharisees were dumb struck, because they could not imagine that anyone would question what Caesar could not have, because anything he demanded was his. The same "Roman lex" structure exists today. We are taxed on so many issues; we cannot discern the differences of what tribute are Caesar's and of which we tithe God. I think, we do not protest enough to know the difference, and our political character suffers the lash. Our generalship lacks knowledge and turns to frustration, worry and at times weaponry.

The W-4 is a simple contract of magnified proportion to the "natural born citizen." The most important aspect of this and other like instruments is what makes them enforceable.

Uniform Commercial Code 3-104.(1), it must be a writing signed by the maker or drawer; The signing must be knowingly, willingly, intentionally and "unconditionally" given, at 3-104.2. What happens when you add a "condition" or covenant to agency?

Signing a W-4 draws the enforcement powers of Admiralty police power, because you waive your personam rights and are now domestic product, and "subject matter" only. Being subject to the "inferior" Article 1 courts; you may as well be a soldier, because the GI cannot reserve "in-personam" Rights and must stand at court martial and challenge subject matter only.

Black's Law. Uniform Code. Many states have adopted the Uniform Code of Military Justice, and others have adopted acts substantially following the Uniform Code.

A state needs the code of Military Justice to obtain police powers. Article III Citizens are summoned by Thee People at probable cause. A policeman, sworn to do their duty to the subject Citizen, may upon proper Grand Jury indictment, bring you before Thee People.

Article II Executive Commander In Chief "executes" statute of Article I, which requires an "unconditional" contractual system that does not advocate due process in the structured and coordinated manner as the Constitution dictates for Citizens of Thee Bill of Rights.

The states are a "forum" government of the United States, which "makes" it a State or Territrorial, "prize" of Admiralty and relies on the 14th Amendment for due process. The "forum" is attempting to erase all the state lines and consolidate Thee People for our "benefit" and/or protection. The various Departments try you without resort to Tribunal because you have agreed by contract and Admiralty is the best Police Power the states can find for quick resolution of issues of reasonable cause. The burden of proof is on the citizen "of interest" via presumption of guilt and innocence must rebut or "dishonor" is issue.

The IRS, DMV, DEA, FBI, banks, schools, HMOs, ferret hunters, and municipalities are all "engrafted" to each other by the "Penumbra Doctrine," which is Federalist "Public Policy." Agency may be estoppel, BUT the individual Sovereign Citizen, when applicable to them, must reserve rights or a "fair and impartial trial" may delict from your corporate neighbor as juror of false judgments.

The Admiralty courts are operated to administer subject matter jurisdiction only, because you waived in personam Rights via contract, "tacit" approval, or by "dishonoring" presentment. Bring up Sovereignty through the UC Codes and the "inferior court" of Article I must yield to Article III Judiciary for a trial of your "peers" based upon reasonable cause.

I have not filed an income tax return since 1978. There is no statute of limitations on non-filers. The IRS and the State of California followed my social security number until 1995. I paid more $500.00 frivolous fines than anyone I know because I signed under penalties of perjury without reserving rights. I made an "unconditional" signing on a W-4, which "made liable" a "promise" as a corporation citizen. I wrote exempt and corporations cannot obtain such status; that is why I was fined. A "frivolous" signing took away my personam Rights and transferred them to the "subject matter" only jurisdiction of "sworn personnel" at in personam.

United States Citizens or "persons" are artificial citizens and agency does not know the difference until you explain it to them in their own language within the UC Code. Myriads of fact fighting, jurisdictional challenges and study material fell upon deaf ears. Property liens were filed in registrar's offices in the hopes I would acquire property in the state "district" I was "residing." Bank accounts were raided and property taken by the "implied power" of statute lex.

In 1991 I studied a few pages from the work of Howard Freeman on the Uniform Commercial Code. I started using the UCC to answer agency demands and began to understand why these "implied powers" had not put me in prison. I could not break Article I statute law until I dishonored their presentments or filed a return or perjured myself. I am an Article III citizen and I made the controversy a Separation of Powers issue.

I found that I did not waive rights when I signed agreements "without prejudice." The only "implied" jurisdiction of agency had been presumptive and I "rebutted." I did not have the proper key of knowledge to fit the political lock until I was successful. The W-4 was frivolous because there was no reservation of my personam rights as prima facie on the instrument that represented Article I with Article II forum procedure. Once I started answering the various agencies properly, they knew I was not domestic product or "subject to public policy" and left me alone, completely. Agency hath no control over Propria Persona unless you waive by contract. The presentment notices stopped and I am exempt without even a thank you for clearing the matter. When my W-2 arrives, I sign my name to it and put "without prejudice" UCC 1-207 above my writing and send it certified mail to the agency. It is proclivity of your adversary not to answer and they did not and they cannot. My life is free from the worry and Jesus is closer than he has ever been with his protective Grace. Thee best insurance you can get, and it's free, with a lot of counsel prayer.

Black's law 5th. False return. To constitute civil or criminal fraud under the Internal Revenue laws, such falsity must be intentional. Mitchell v. C.I.R., C.C.A.Ga., 118 F.2d 308.

Perjury is the beast of agency and the "promise" brings the executor to collect per contract. A reservation of Rights "vitiates" perjury and cannot "sustain a promise."

UCC 3-104. it must contain an (2) unconditional; A soldier "must" contract unconditionally and waive in-personam because he is government "issue." The politics of this act cannot be stressed enough, because We Thee People are victims of this same voluntary signing of contract. Make the instrument "conditional" and the power of enforcement is lost by agency, in the majority of issues. A sovereign cannot be a soldier if he does not wish to sign his Rights away to the government. Agency activity cannot subjugate the non-corporate individual. An instrument made "conditional" does not comply with the enforcement or promise at UCC 3-104.3 and abates executor. The intended party must retain its enforceable status and character "unconditionally," or the instrument is vitiated along with perjury.

Black's. Commercial Law. An undertaking to pay and it must be more than an acknowledgment of an obligation. UCC 3-102.1[c].

It must be "unconditional" at the signing or agency cannot negotiate the instrument at issue. Without Prejudice, UCC 1-207, signed above your signature "will not sustain a promise" or an "appearance." Without any of the above, enumerated sections of the UCC, the instrument is "dead in law." Article I Legislative makes the statutes, which are then departmental at Article II Executive/Admiralty, which implements the codes. We the People are "entitled" to Article III judicial and must declare or loose the Bill of Rights.

Black's. Law. A concurrent or joint resolution of legislature is not "a law," Koenig v. Flynn, 258 N.Y. 292, 179 N.E. 705, 707; Ward v. State, 176 Okl. 368, 56 P.2d 136, 137; a resolution of the House of Representatives is not a "law," State ex rel. Todd v. Yelle, 7 Wash.2d 443, 110 P.2d 162, 165; an unconstitutional statute is not a "law," Flournoy v. First Nat. Bank of Shreveport, 197 La. 1067, 3 So.2d 244, 248. That which must be obeyed and followed by citizens subject to sanctions or legal consequences is a law. Law is the will of the supreme power of the state. Calif. Civil Code 22.1.

Calif. Government Code 22.2, "The Common Law of England, so far as it is not repugnant to or inconsistent with the Constitution of the united States, or the Constitution or the laws of this state, is the rule of decision in all the courts of this state." "All Laws which are repugnant to the Constitution are null and void." Marbury v. Madison 5 U.S. 137, 174, 176. "Where rights secured by the Constitution are involved, there can be no rule making or legislation which would abrogate them." Miranda v. Arizona, 384 U.S. 436 p. 491. "The claim and exercise of a Constitutional Right cannot be converted into a crime." Miller v. U.S. "No one is bound to obey an unconstitutional law and no courts are bound to enforce it." 16 Am Jur 2d, 177, late Am Jur 2d 256.

The only citizens "subject" to statutes are those found within the "territory" of the 14th Amendment or municipalities contracted to that instrument. Thee Sovereign Citizen who contracts "unconditionally" with government activity are "unconscionably" seduced by the representing agency and must rebut or suffer unconscionable actions.

Black's 5th pg. 1264, "Statutes are confined to their own territory, and have no extraterritorial effect."

Article I Section 8 Clause 17 defines the jurisdiction of the statute "inferior courts" and "implied powers" of the Federal Government over artificial and contracted citizens of corporate status. We Thee People are "extraterritorial" within our separate state and agency must be may be abated with a non-assumpsit, voluntary signing.

"Because of what appear to be Lawful commands on the surface, many citizens, because of their respect for what appears to be law, are cunningly coerced into waiving their rights, due to ignorance." U.S. v. Miller, 350 U.S. 179, 187.

A Sovereign Citizen cannot loose Rights, but you can waive them, or allow boards, municipalities and "corporate America" to vote them away. Look at any signing as a waiver of your most precious personam Rights and reserve them. Most "government activity" contracts are de facto and void of "benefit." "Public Law" signs its Citizens au masse in hopes of obtaining the presumptive compliance from all citizens regardless of status.

Article I Section 2 Clause 3: "Representatives and direct taxes shall be apportioned among the several states which may be included within this Union, according to their respective numbers."

I will not bore you with excises, direct, imposts, duties or indirect tax procedures. The income tax is a graduated form of direct tax and de facto to the Sovereign state Citizen unless you are a good little volunteer and validate agency presumption by acquiescence to their jurisdiction "unconditionally" and "must be signed under penalty of perjury."

The heart of the institution of taxing lies with the W-4 as a corporate negotiable "unit." Your job application is agency's first look at its new corporate for benefit citizen. You admit to being corporate by your social security number and the little box you checked asking if you are a U.S. Citizen. The only "benefit" is the insurance; a corporate property will not hire you without your being insured. From that point on, justice is blind, and Thee Citizen bears the presumptive burden of being mugged on payday and incorporated to his Lawful stand.

Prior to our signing our political lives away to domestic product and government activity, We Thee People were our own individual Sovereign entity. Congress puts together all activity the states use to subjugate its Sovereign Citizens to artificial culture and the President hires the

Department heads. The "Penumbra Doctrine" heads then put forth the myriads of codes and procedures, and we sign on to follow the "persons" ahead of us. The enrollment contracts we conduct our daily lives with are not unconstitutional because we voluntarily put our hand to the instruments. The units are cleverly worded as to their "forum" and seem innocent enough, which allows us to incorporate unconditionally at the time of the writing.

The above stated UCC 3-104 is for corporate use and adds "limited liability" to the natural person if we reserve our "personam." Agency "situs" signed you up as an "artificial" U.S. Citizen found under the 14th Amendment due process. Open season on your Sovereignty is declared if you sign the document without reserving your Rights on the face of the instrument or W-4. This makes the unit "dead in law" for it vitiates the unit and is not then a promise with criminal connotations. The code must be read in harmony with your Sovereign entity as intercede through Thee Bill of Rights under UCC 1-103.6. Persons born in Territories are not Sovereign Citizens, but U.S. Citizens. Hawaii is now a state under siege for its wealth, because agency is waiving the same forum contracts We Thee People signed before Hawaii became a state. Posterity is a moot issue without Sovereignty and Covenant.

We must pray for Thee People of Hawaii, I am certain they miss their Sovereignty the most for they are new at struggling without personam Covenant. If Puerto Rico could have Thee Knowledge of what a real state is like, they would not have voted down statehood. Puerto Rico is a Territory and "subject to the jurisdiction thereof" the United States at Article I Section 8 Clause 17.

"Income taxes statutes apply only to state created creatures known as corporations no matter whether state, local, or federal.", Colonial Pipeline Co. v. Traigle, 421 US 100.

The Sovereign is free to contract as the spirit moves it. We must blend with the "wolf" to keep from having to fight him. To do this we must be as "wise as the serpent." Reserving our Rights leaves the beast "as gentle as the dove," because we do not have to occupy the cross and our generalship will provide Grace by relieving our worry.

"State created creatures" also walk, talk and sign unconscionable agreements without reserving their Rights. The state cannot give you the knowledge of their sovereignty, for it would mean their demise.

"The employer is not authorized to alter the form or to dishonor the employees claim." The W-4 is automatic with its enumerated application per IRS Code 3402 (f) (3) and U.S. v. Malinowski, 347 F. Supp. 352.

If you do not exempt yourself properly, you will find out quickly who the boss wolf is and a $500 frivolous will follow without trial. Agency can only do that with help from Admiralty and the police power you created by an "unconditional" signing. No agent hath the power to change your reservation, because it would be a breach of contract and a violation of Thee Separate Powers, because "the IRS has no interest between the employee and the employer and the IRS has no interest in the circumstances of the action… and is not a party." Stahoviak v. Denver and the RGW

Railroad Co. # 79CV205, Rout County, Colorado. "There is no legal requirement to file a W-4 form." U.S. v. John Freeman, 81-CR-112-U.S.D. Wisconsin.

The "affirmative defense" is not difficult to learn and will serve Thee People with political Liberties in their quest for the Bill of Rights promised within Thee Constitution of these united States of America.

The W-4 unit states; "Under penalties of perjury, I certify that I am entitled to the number of withholding allowances claimed on this certificate, or I am entitled to claim exempt status;" Employee's signature; Form is not valid unless you sign it."

Reserve your Rights, "Without Prejudice" UCC 1-207, above your signature becomes "prima facie" evidence that you are "express" in reserving your Rights. One of those Rights is the will to contract or not. Feel free to write EXEMPT in the square. A non- "assumpsit" cannot be "certified" as a contract or privilege license.

The IRS will tell you that you can claim more or less dependants, depending on how much you wish to pay into your "fund." At the end of the filing period, you must claim the proper amount on your return or another penalty of perjury rears its ugly head. Sounds like a catch 22 to this Sovereign Citizen, and I will have none of it. The "fund" is their's, and the burden of proof is on you under penalty of perjury if you wish to have any portion of the refund returned. When rights are reserved prima facie, you will not suffer a penalty for agency would now be in violation of its own charter with the Executive. If you do file a return, RESERVE your rights, because you are "made liable" per statute. It would be interesting to see an agent dare audit an instrument that is non-negotiable, because perjury does not exist.

Black's Law 5th. Certificate. A written assurance, or official representation, that some act has or has not been done, or some event occurred, or some legal formality has been complied with. A statement of some fact in a writing signed by the party certifying. A declaration in writing.

The form mentions the fact that you may claim exemption, but the argument is; if you are a corporation, you cannot file an exemption. Agency only knows what you tell them. So far, you have told them you are a corporate entity and "made liable" by statute. To be "entitled," is where the serpent meets the Sovereign. Isn't it nice of the IRS to give you the right to reclaim your money from your very own "fund?"

Black's. Entitle. In its usual sense, to entitle is to give a right or legal title to. Schmidt v. Gibbons, 101 Ariz. 222, 418 P.2d 378, 380. To qualify for; to furnish with proper grounds for seeking or claiming. In ecclesiastical law, to entitle is to give a title or ordination as a minister.

The UCC prepares the way for the entitlement of exemption at agency via the W-4. I need no entitlement from human kind to teach Thee Law of God, and Thee Truth and Grace of Jesus Christ. With "reservation" the burden of proof is upon agency.

Black's. Entitlement. Right to benefits, income or property which may not be abridged without due process.

IRS due process is nonexistent; this wolf is strictly Admiralty by contract and a "government activity" by definition. Presumptive agency activity is as avoidable as a self-inflicted hanging, if your rights are reserved. What more could We Thee People ask for?

There are two types of due process. The 5th Amendment, which keeps the Federal Government out of your liberty and the other, is the 14th Amendment, which protects Federal Statutes in regards to contracting state Sovereign citizens to its procedural due process. Give me Liberty or give me a way out of domestic subjectivity and We Thee People will prosper, so help us God. The "forum" unit is not valid unless you sign "unconditionally." There is no promise, assumpsit, obligation, or negotiable unit to cause an issue of perjury.

After the exemption, "Federal jurisdiction cannot be assumed, but must be clearly shown." Brooks v. Yawkey 200 F. 2d. 633. "The law requires proof of jurisdiction to appear on the record of the administrative agency and all administrative proceedings." Hagans v. Lavine, 415 U.S. 533.

The escape clause at federal prosecution for Sovereign Citizens of the states is Rule 12. Defenses and Objections- (b) "…The following defenses may at the option of the pleader be made by motion: (1) lack of jurisdiction over the subject matter. (2) lack of jurisdiction over the person. A motion making any of these defenses shall be made before pleading… (h) (3) "Whenever it appears by suggestion of the parties or otherwise that the court lacks jurisdiction of the subject matter, the court shall dismiss the action."

Before pleading is the time to "answer" any inquiry of your adversary and to declare Propria Persona. Even a jury summons is a trap by asking you about hardship for non-compliance of jury duty. An answer gives jurisdiction to the agency because you give "tacit" approval to the tribunal so they may exercise their presumption of your cooperation. Do not feel threatened by these types of "summons;" the wolf is presumptively stalking for a stray. If you feel threatened, "without prejudice" UCC 1-207 will reserve your rights and point out several issues to agency that are very difficult to overcome. Like the selective service and the IRS, they only know what you volunteer to them. The rest is none of their business. Only artificial Citizens may be "drafted" to do anything. Reserve all your Rights on any and every piece of correspondence that comes before you, if you are in a compromise situation where a signing is under duress.

"His [the attorney's] first duty is to the court, not to the client, and wherever the duties he owes to the client conflict with the duties he owes to the court, as an officer of the court in the administration of justice, the former must yield to the latter." Corpus Juris Secundum, Attorney & Client, Sec. 4, pg 802.

Your lawyer will not explain his elliptical duty to you, for if he did you would have no part of him. When the Sovereign Citizen is exempt by code, the burden of proof reverts to agency to prove otherwise, for the presumption that the citizen is not exempt, has been rebutted.

The IRS and other agency's make their living on presentments, which are "dishonored" by the Citizen. Lawyers are working under the same Article II procedure as the court; all have something to gain by your compliance and are not shy in asserting their contracted rights.

Black's. Presentment. Presentment is a demand for acceptance or payment made upon the maker, acceptor, drawee or other payor by or on behalf of the holder. UCC 3-504.1.

A contract usually exists before the Sovereign gets a presentment. A missed payment, court date or presumptive misunderstanding of intent may become actionable. If you did not knowingly, willingly and intentionally sign for the instrument, protect yourself with the code. An unanswered presumption of owing money is as good as a contract if the citizen "dishonors" the sum demanded. Do not throw a presentment into the garbage where it belongs, for you "dishonor" the instrument by failing to rebut and the obligation will not be impaired.

Black's law. Dishonor. To refuse to accept or pay a draft or to pay a promissory note when duly presented. An instrument is dishonored when a necessary or optional presentment is duly made and due acceptance or payment is refused, or cannot be obtained within the prescribed time, or in case of bank collections, the instrument is seasonably returned by the midnight deadline or presentment is excused and the instrument is not duly accepted or paid. UCC 3-507.1; 4-210.

All the holder needs to get you to their court is for you to disregard the bill or instrument. The court will see you have failed to answer or refuse to pay and give the creditor default to your pocketbook or garnishment. Always answer agencies, do not "fail to answer" their claims for this act alone will cause you worry. Give them only the reservation of Rights "virus;" nothing else is their business.

A state Citizen must force agency to use the mail, not the phone. You cannot build your "administrative record" with "parol" evidence. A dishonored claim is a presumptive admission of guilt, and that alone gives the presentment credibility in the eye of the "trier of fact." Your answer or reservation of rights should be short, "without prejudice" UCC 1-207 will do nicely and will speak volumes to "public policy." Return within 72 hours, via certified mail.

There are several answers a "vigilant" Citizen may use as study to presentments within these treatise, which I repeat again and on occasion, AGAIN, and least we forget, highlight all reservation of Rights phrases, an agent will test your knowledge. I think the Truth bears repeating.

UCC 1-207.9 states; "When a waivable right or claim is involved, the failure to make a reservation thereof, causes a loss of the right, and bars its assertion at a later date."

More Truth; as soon as the opportunity arises for you to reserve your rights, DO IT even if you have doubts, because it is the best insurance you can get. I was an insurance agent once upon a time, but never sold a policy. I learned very quickly that the business would not make my family prosper for reasons I will not share. A presentment is as powerful from the insurance agency as it is from any IRS agent or a neighbor who presumes you owe money and makes a civil claim.

Answer every presumed debt as if you know what you are doing. If you do not owe money or wise agency to "verify," the first presentment may be answered; "I hereby refute the validity of your unattested presentment/claim, without dishonor, I do not owe this money." Sign, date, and write "without prejudice" UCC 1-207 on the face of the presentment demand, above your signature. Affix a certified post number to the "prima facie," which now becomes an evidence document for the trier of fact, and proves you are "express" in attempting to work out verification of the agency demand. Mail the demand to the agent via return receipt requested.

The individual agent is on "notice" that you are not waiving any rights and you want the instrument verified. The agent will then need to swear an oath that the presentment is a legitimate "true bill," or find another fool who will commit perjury to do so. The Common Law does not sue out the entire state or agency, it becomes more personal and the agent must use great caution. The next presentment may be a request for confirmation of your "protest" or any other subterfuge indicating agency does not understand your demand. The presentment may be from a different collection agency that has bought the supposed debt. The more third party intervention the better, because the weakness becomes more apparent and much harder to prove, because "the chain of evidence" is broken. The collectors are hoping you fold and start payment or refuse as a means of forcing you to dishonor so they can win by default. If the same agency persist, return the instrument with a copy of the above stated "without dishonor" statement and a UCC 3-505.

I have never had an agency answer this, not even an insurance agent or banker, and they are better trained at fleecing the Sovereign Citizen than the IRS. The Rights of Thee Sovereign Citizen can be violated by this conjecture. Agency activity is constructed very well and the individual sworn "person" must use caution, for ONLY now may your Rights be violated. You have notified an agent of your intent to protect yourself and require a "verified" instrument if one can be had. Proclivity by the individual agent is the wise choice, for it is his hide that will hang in the patriot's den if he does not have a true negotiable instrument. Many promotions are had by how quickly an agent can get a citizen to pay an unjust bill. If he does come up with a verified bill, work out a solution on better terms. A trial at the Common Law must be had to prove the fact that you owe anything over $20.00 and criminal intent must be proved. Using the codes will give back due process of Thee Bill of Rights, instead of the due process of the 14th Amendment.

DO NOT ADD TO THIS COUNTER DEMAND.

UCC 3-505.4 Counter demands by party to whom presentment is made.
The party to whom presentment is made may, without dishonor, require:
[a] Exhibition of the instrument (creating the liability).
[b] Reasonable identification of the person making presentment and evidence of his authority to make it if made for another; and

[c] That the instrument be produced for acceptance or payment at a place specified in it, or if there be none, at any place reasonable in the circumstances; and

[d] A signed receipt of the instrument for any partial or full payment and its surrender on full payment.

Failure to comply with any such requirement invalidates the presentment, but the person presenting has a reasonable time in which to comply and the time for acceptance or payment runs from the time of compliance.

NOTICE: UCC 1-201(26)
From:
Domicile:
city:
Non-Domestic

CERTIFIED MAIL post#

Government Activity Agent: Restatement, Second, Agency {9}

At address:

I AM, an Article III, Preamble Citizen of the California Republic. Your "implied powers" instrument "note," is not "assignable" or "negotiable" under UCC 3-104. I find this document Unconscionable UCC 2-302. I do not and will not accept, the liability associated with a "compelled" agreement of any unrevealed commercial benefit, or "Penumbra Doctrine" "engraft."

My "conditional" "representation" is "without prejudice" UCC1-207 and is affirmed to the instrument herein as Exhibit "A". Article III, at UCC 1-103.6, The Statute, being enforced as a commercial obligation of a commercial agreement, must now be construed in HARMONY with the COMMON LAW. No statute precludes this Citizen from seeking redress at the united States Supreme Court. In order to recover in federal court through [1983], plaintiff must show that a federal constitutional right was violated and the individual violating that constitutional right did so "under color of law." 42 U.S.C.A 1983.

You have 30 days to answer the above-described Notice. UCC 1-201(10). If you have a right to assert, it is your duty to speak. Your "silence" is, "estoppel" in pais.

"without prejudice" UCC I-207

Citizen_____

Chapter 5: Internal Revenue Service - Title 26

These three words strike fear into some of the best "freedom fighters" that I have ever met. The Patriot Community is stretched far and wide on meaning of facts the I.R.S. represents. I have found that once you are "within" the contractual structure of this monolithic corporation, you are obligated to do as you "promised" at UCC 3-104.3. There is no amount of research and fact fighting that will help. The answer for me was to stay "without" the facts and instead rely on Thee Law. The W-4 is the beginning of this Penumbra and I have found a way to extricate myself from the contractual structure that dispossesses you, once you sign it. Our employers insist we join the marriage of corporate America and the IRS, so I give signature to the W-4 instrument, in a special way. This signing is done without the gnashed teeth, for the clenched fist gathers no writing implement!

After prying open a couple of fingers, just enough to sign "Without Prejudice" UCC 1-207 above my signature, I then filled the little square box which has eluded me for so long with EXEMPT. Social security number is optional, and may lawfully be left blank, the little squares filled with N/A, because it is none of the IRS business how many dependants I have or whether or not I am married or single. HMO's, workmen's compensation, unemployment, ad nauseam, are all separate corporate "nature," and required for your and corporate protection. The W-4 is not a "lawful" state Citizen document unless voluntarily signed at UCC 3-104.1, and the "unconditional" signing at UCC 3-104.2 is your clue to run to the Bill of Rights for Remedy at UCC 1-103.6., which leaves "promise" "in want" of contract. Personam is your personal property; to sign to another to possess is in personam. A volunteer makes an excellent foot stool to agency mischief and police power is provided for "benefit."

The "without prejudice" statement vitiates the contractual structure of the signing and does not sustain any promise as to future conditions, as it is non-assumpsit, not voluntary and conditioned. Get out your dictionaries, you need to understand this before you open your fist to sign any agreement with agency.

We Thee People have attempted to love the IRS for over 40 years in this "domestic war" of educational subjugation and 'social engineering." The IRS relentless pursuit of us who know there is a way out of this mess has been tireless. There are many who have protected themselves very well, and there are those who have served time in the "corporate American" prisons due to their own ignorance of individual political status, bless their hearts!

Many of those who have found a 'solution" to the myriad of facts hidden within the blue smoke and mirrors of this most high Article I corporation, keep the information close to their pocketbooks. Others of the Patriot community produce false witness and information for thousands of dollars, and we find ourselves surrounded again and again by the agents and officers of Article II/Admiralty-Police Power, after Article I Legislative/Statute has had its way, by convincing the democratic majority through "public policy," that all are subject to tribute.

Admiralty is the contractual access by which the people may be scourged, BUT we must individually be "made liable" by contract. Without assenting signature, Title 26 at the IRS Code is irresponsible, unconscionable and has no police power of state Citizens. Who, What, When, Where, Why and How is an investigative tool to ferret out this many headed beast, of the "Penumbra Doctrine," infra [Black's. Law 5th].

WHO

WHO is required to file and income tax return or a tax statement and WHO are the IRS? "All persons made liable" are required per the IRS Privacy provision.

We Thee People, those Natural Born Citizens of a Preamble Free Republican state are exempt by birthright under Thee promise of Thee New 'sovereign Covenant" and Constitution. I am, as God is, of Law, and my mortal soul is forfeit if this teaching were false. My own personal covenant with Jesus is my counsel, and I worship the same as you. I do not go to an "organized" church as you may, which is a separate issue, and I will not cover that here, well maybe, just a little. Thee Church is not required to license, nor fill out forms for the IRS to "allow" a "non-profit exemption." God sings lead in Thee Peoples Church, and a license to teach "Thee New Covenant" of Jesus Christ is a Separation of Powers issue. The Shepherd is to Teach with "authority," not Law.

You stand on the same God given ground as I, and you are protected under Article III and the Bill of Rights, as your Church may be. Other nations are forfeiting of this Right due to their own ignorance, or failure to have a bigger "staff" of Law to protect their status as Shepherd of thee free Citizens.

Mammon is among us all as the "wolf." We Thee People are the "sheep among" them. When we gather at an issue, we set ourselves up for failure, because IRS facts/Penumbra are confusing and very little Law can be found "within" any statute unless you are "made liable" by "dishonor." When you are subject within the statute jurisdiction of Article I, as are those persons from another nation who are artificial by statute and/or corporate diversity, you must comply or be destroyed by the power of taxation and subjectivity.

The IRS is a Constitutional entity under the 14th Amendment, Article I, and 16th Amendment not withstanding. Article II furnishes the Admiralty "implied" "inferior court" police power that you authorized at signature.

To tax the Sovereign Citizen or those state Citizens protected under Article III Judiciary, the IRS requires the contractual W-4 agreement. Maritime charter demands unconditional signing, because Rule 12(b), in personam jurisdiction is required. The Judiciary would have something to say via Separation of Powers Doctrine if IRS were to tax an unsigned state Citizen. Demur the W-4 contract and the IRS is "without" their jurisdiction and cannot interfere with "obligation of contract" at Article I Section 10 Clause 1 and "Privileges and immunities of Citizens in the several states" at Article IV Section 2 Clause 1. The IRS is a corporate tax and a Constitutional issue is also raised at Article 1 Section 2 Clause 3; "Representatives and direct taxes shall be apportioned." There is not a conceivable way agency can breathe life into the W-4 Phoenix once you have crashed it in the flames of its corporate origin.

The individual at Acts 22:25 has the Power of Christ and Thee Law has been written so mankind cannot cover its Truth, and by Grace go We Thee People. Nothing can come between you and your Sovereign Lord. The only thing that does is CONTRACT with agency, and once this is done improperly, Mammon and the seduction spirit prevails. When we contract, we do so individually, your mother, and friends may not stand with you when the day comes to pay to Caesar what is not his. We as a Free People reach out to others for petition, redress and protection as our instinctive qualities and natural inner compass dictate, "Without" counsel with God. When we do this, in ignorance, it is a "prayer" to mammon, and even within this great Nation we are beguiled within the jurisdiction of our own compliance through "devise" and false teaching.

How do we as individuals seek the knowledge of our own personal Sovereign? Paul of Tarsus did so at Acts 22:25; "Is it lawful for you to scourge a man that is a Roman, and not condemned?" What made Paul different from other men? Paul was a state Citizen of Rome. Paul used his knowledge of "competent Law counsel" with Jesus to provide his "sovereign Exemption" at punishment of a victimless crime. State oppressor must prove jurisdiction when challenged, even if you are a conquered Nation.

The State of Rome was demanding loyalty to the Pharisees so Paul would stop teaching, but Paul had his duty to perform in Jesus name and he stated the words of his Sovereign Counsel.

The burden of proof was put upon Paul as it is to this day at Law of presumption and inferior courts of the IRS type agency. Paul successfully rebutted the presumption that he was subject to the Roman Lex Law at Christian domestication, which is the Civil Liberties of Lex law at this writing. Only in Lex/Roman Law is there a separation of church and State. The Constitution does not contain this language. This usage can be found within the 14th Amendment, statutes of Congress and the de facto counsel of the Supreme Court, when dealing with its corporate "persons" using "needful buildings."

The Sovereign child Citizen is in personam at the enrollment of "public policy" contract in "social engineering" school. The enrollment signature must contain the above "reservation of rights" or your child looses their state Citizenship and becomes subject to "scourging," because they waived their "personam" Rights with an "unconditional" signing at UCC 3-104.2. The schoolyard MP's and the W-4 instrument are of the same master and a reservation of Rights must be upon the unit. "Dishonor" of agreement must come by "crime" with "probable cause," instead of failure to do or not to do a "thing" which will make you "reasonable cause" and actionable in personam. We Thee People are "entitled" to Thee Bill of Rights, not guaranteed, the individual must ask by giving "notice."

Paul was a Sovereign Citizen of Rome; this "affirmative defense" was impossible for the Romans to overcome, because the burden of proof was with the individual Roman guard to verify, that is why the guard was frightened, he found he was about to wrongfully flog a state Citizen. A "verified Administrative Law Remedy" was put before the Roman soldier that had repercussions throughout the Lex Empire; because Paul's personal appeal sustained his "personam" status. Paul proclaimed his Sovereignty as an "affirmative defense," and was then protected by the same Lex Law, which had orders to persecute him. Now, with an army, to keep the Pharisees from having him killed, Paul was guarded away by his captors.

Paul of Tarsus was an individual, as you and I are. He was sent "far into the Gentiles" to teach the word of Law, that we are blessed to have in America today. Our Lord said, "that they [gentiles] will hear it," Acts 28:28. Thee Constitution of These united States is the "New Covenant," and is the scribe of Paul through Gods own hand. Truth and Grace of Jesus is on this land as the Prophets have foretold. By the natural law of God, will we prosper, or fall to mammon by waiving our Natural Law Rights, whether by contract or "tacit" with our heads bowed to the liege of "benefit" and seductive spirit.

All Nations began with these inner body compass Rights as citizens, but power, greed and devise usurped their sovereignty. Article III and Thee Bill of Rights are the Law of the natural born found within Article II Section I Clause [5] of Thee Constitution of these united States of America. All others are "artificial" by statute, United States Citizens or have waived their personam freedom to Lex, such as military code of justice and "corporate America" jurisprudence at public policy.

WHO is the IRS? Article II Executive issue at Maritime contract with police power built within for your in personam control. The 14th Amendment gives the best clue to "residency" tax status within the "residency" jurisdiction of the United States Government. The 14th Amendment is the result of the greatest usurpation and deception of individual Sovereign Rights known to mankind since the birth of this Republic. Who We Thee People are depends on how we signature our covenants, because of our diverse citizenship status.

The 14th Amendment was ratified in 1868, and is not Law for any state Citizen. Those U.S. Citizens found within a state remain a resident of the United States for domestic police and tax purposes. The 16th Amendment became Law for U.S. Citizens in 1913. Constitutional guarantees remain intact for no Article III or Bill of Rights laws were abrogated. IRS power is "implied" and becomes factual law ONLY at unconditional signature on W-4.

14th Amendment; All persons born or naturalized in the United States, and subject to the jurisdiction thereof, are citizens of the United States and of the State wherein they reside.

"All persons," is a give away to the whole corporate "culture." We Thee People, are born individually, we have however, multiple citizenship status and must have knowledge of which jurisdictional claims are applicable at any given time to protect our political state Citizenship. Diversity status is of a Preamble citizen born in a Republican free state with Thee Bill of Rights and Article III Judiciary as intercede when not waived per contracted police power. Alien status is contractual United States citizenship at Article I/Legislative and Article II/Executive Admiralty and Article1 Section 8 Clause 17, which overshadows even the most wary of Patriots. U.S. Citizens are registered with the government and are "artificial," corporate and subject to their master, Congress. These "persons" are transient from other Nations and joined at the Admiralty flag, as is a soldier, per contract.

Your local bank, stocks, insurance companies, real estate, motor vehicles, fishing license, wills, HMO's, ferret hunters, police state officers and your child's school, claim you as U. S. Citizen and subject per negotiable contract. Insurance companies are "born" "subject" as multiple "persons" and are within the jurisdiction of 1-8-17. The difference being, Article III Judicial and Thee Bill of Rights are individual, personal Rights. Contractual agreements between corporate "partners" for benefit are alien to a political personam and the Bill of Rights must be reserved or lost. Our Rights to keep and bear arms, spend our hard earned wages on our families instead of bailing out United States, worship God in our schools, and have ferrets as property in California, are all victims of the same citizenship status, requiring the individual to stand for himself and demand Sovereign status at issue.

Civil Liberties are statute and "engrafted" from the Bill of Rights so the people will be fooled easily into thinking their rights are still intact, although waived through de facto statute, and doled out as commercial benefit. These so called Civil Liberties are engrafted by the same implied, presumptive powers of the "Penumbra Doctrine". Natural persons or ignorant Sovereign citizens of "sovereign Covenant" who are enticed to enter the inferior courts are misguided in their trust of agency devise and police power. The Natural born have a pure and personal covenant of Law with the first breath of life. The "artificial" "persons" of the 14th Amendment are those of corporate, municipal, and alien status and are regulated as such because they are within the jurisdiction of the statute "chartered" by Congress at Title 26, as the creator of the IRS. We are regulated, only per contract and must realize the difference in Heritage and character or suffer the same fate as other Peoples of Nations who have forgiven their heritage to educated representation of false teaching and must forever withstand agency seduction benefit.

Corporations are not "within" Gods Law, and therefore have no character. We Thee People are forfeiting our character and citizenship, if we do not intervene in our own Propria Persona. By not waiving our Rights, in our own defense and protection at Law in an Article III forum, we keep our personam intact and police power is abated. Otherwise, we may fall victim to being "a person of interest" or actually believe the Patriot Act applies to us.

We are personally contracted and responsible to our individual New Covenant Creator, unless we waive Thee individual Bill of Rights and allow agency as intercede by statute.

"A judicial process operating in personam, and requiring person to whom it is directed to do or refrain from doing a particular thing." Gainsburg v. Dodge, 193 Ark.473, 101 S.W.2d 178, 180. Fed.R.Civil P. 65.

Contract is the only way you can be refrained from doing anything that does not victimize or have criminal intent against another natural person. Thee Golden Rule of Jesus are applicable within the Constitution. A contract would be vitiated, if signed at repugnance, or which would be an "absurdity" to the Constitution, or prevent clarity at Law. The State cannot be a victim if the criterion at the 10th Amendment is met. The People of Grand Jury cannot be called to represent "revenue" matters of corporate "action" or "federal constitutional" issues. An appearance on a jury must not judge these matters or false witness is manifest. A jury should hear crime issues only.

Black's. "The action in personam is that which we sue him who is under obligation to us to do something or give something."

For all purposes of law, Thee People should consider all Article I and Article II agency courts of statute, which are "inferior" to Article III Judicial, as Federal courts. The Admiralty flag is the clue. When We Thee People stand or sign contracts before a flag with the gold fringe we have waived our sovereign personam to Federal citizenship and all that remains is "subject matter" jurisdiction, where the burden of proof is "presumptively" ours to prove innocence.

We owe nothing to no one unless by contract at "accord and satisfaction," which results in a voluntary obligation. If these contracts are intentional, knowing, and willingly given, then pay the due, if not, and fraud is apparent, do not take the lash for sin is an encumbrance upon the spirit and worry your effort.

WHAT

WHAT has "made liable" Thee People? Signing any corporate agreement unconditionally, namely the W-4 or other covenant, which subjects in personam to negotiable unit, and you are "made liable." Thee Sovereign "New Covenant," or Lex, one or the other, will judge your ignorance. Which Law of mankind will represent you? Roman Lex does not require a victim, or any criminal intent to exact tax or police power "action" upon Thee People. We Thee People inherited Truth and Grace of Law as Sovereign, though many have been scourged and imprisoned because we do not claim "entitlement."

All will go by Christ, if the Golden Law is followed. Those who follow mammon will discover, painfully, that We Thee People cannot follow two masters. WHAT, we seek depends entirely upon our individual citizenship status, the ignorance scale, political contract ability and our Generalship at controversy.

Those persons "made liable" per the IRS "Privacy Act" must file the 1040 or tax statement. Did you as an individual, instead of relying upon a "guru," or educational teacher, ever consider what the words made liable actually mean? To be "made liable" is something you do to yourself, per contract with agency. Words matter a great deal. Our brain is the most powerful weapon we possess. Our hands do battle, make peace and sign "unconditional" contracts at orders from our knowledge base. When our educational values supercede our political knowledge, chaos ensues and treachery abounds, for we are our brother's keeper.

Black's. Internal. Relating to the interior; comprising within boundary lines; of interior concern or interest; domestic, as opposed to foreign.

Interior is "within" the jurisdiction of the issue, covenant, or state and boundaries are established by Thee Law of Constitutional standards that apply to each jurisdiction "within" the authority of the power that is expressed, usually and ordinarily per contract. The interior of the IRS is located within the boundaries of The United States at Article I, Section 8, Clause 17 of the Constitution and is domestic within its Territory and anything foreign or "without" its jurisdiction must be by contract under Executive Maritime forum.

The flag that flies the gold fringe, should serve as warning to all who wish to board and "benefit," that mammon were open to negotiable contract. Thereby the U.S. Citizen of transplant from any nation, corporate, municipal or artificial, domesticates itself to total control and in personam possession by boarding the U.S. vessel of subjugation and is "subject to the jurisdiction thereof" at their own free will, which qualifies agency's corporate police power existence.

Article I Section 8, Clause 17: "To exercise exclusive Legislation in all Cases whatsoever, over such District (not exceeding ten Miles square) as may, by Cession of particular States, and the Acceptance of Congress, become the Seat of the Government of the United States, and to exercise like Authority over all Places purchased by the Consent of the Legislature of the State in which the Same shall be, for the Erection of Forts, Magazines, Arsenals, dockyards, and other needful Buildings;

Article I may ONLY legislate to those "within" the "internal" jurisdiction of the U.S. District, all else is withheld per the 10th Amendment. To sign "within" the federalist jurisdiction, contract or tacit assent must be obtained per Obligation of Contract at Article I Section 10 [1], which justifies agency duress, and police power coercion among those who sign voluntarily at UCC 3-104.1 and are subsequently "made liable". If you wish not to partake of any "benefit" the Congress or state Legislature has to offer, then be careful of what you signature and protect your Bill of Rights with reservation at UCC 1-207, where "no Rights are thereby waived." This puts agency at disadvantage when contract codes and charter do not comply with procedures of the common law at UCC 1-103.6, because the "code must be read in harmony with the Common Law." If there is no contract, there can be no subjugation of our Liberties, if there is no victim, there can be no crime and the state of our domicile has no cause or claim upon the Natural Law of our New Covenant Citizenship within our freeborn status.

Your respective state follows federalist "forum" "Public policy" and passes the same legislative laws as Congress. These state statutes are no more binding than their sister "Penumbra Doctrine" federalist forum. When Rights are reserved, state taxes will also stop, gun control of the citizen will stop, and the ferret killers will have to find a more aggressive pet to slaughter for "want of jurisdiction."

WHEN

WHEN, or at what point in our individual "intercourse" with IRS are We Thee People "made liable"? UPON the signing at UCC 3-104.1, we "must" be extremely cautious, for here lays our Liberties and waivers to them in-personam. The agreement will be followed by agency, which insists that you follow the "unconditional" terms of the agreement to the letter. Our prime political goal at blending with the wolf is the knowledge of the serpent. Is the signing an intentional act or brought upon by duress and, or fraud? The signing is presumed to be a voluntary meeting of the minds, on terms and conditions of the issue. Our jobs, drivers license, bank accounts, contractors license and even enrolling our children in school, is hazardous to our Rights, and waivers abound thereto, because we are ignorant at agency compliance and tolerance is tacit agreement.

The W-4 is the best contract of this sort to explain. Who, in their right mind would sign such an agreement in the first place? You and I, every day of the week, engage agency with our suffrage in ignorance and the inevitable outcome is tribute. The W-4 is the negotiable unit, which gives agency in personam possession obligates for tax purposes. This type of contract is duress and unconscionable in any court at UCC 2-302. With that, consider UCC 3-104.2, which insist the signing be "unconditional," because a condition of without prejudice would vitiate perjury, and will not sustain a "promise" of obligation at UCC 3-104.3. The signing "Without Prejudice" UCC 1-207, directly above our signature would then be a non-assumpsit, which avers, "he did not partake" of the unconscionable act. We sign these units of negotiability to have our job and care for our families. We view the instrument as unavoidable, and to have our peace, we sign in ignorance.

A simple bill of sale with the reservation above the signature will save a ferret by claiming it as property under the Bill of Rights. The contraband laws cannot resort to "taking" without jurisdiction to do so. A trial must be had to prove the state has access to your property and the issue at controversy is more than $20.00, so you ferret lovers must stop calling your little guys pets because the State has de facto jurisdiction over a myriad of animals it considers dangerous. Put the agency to prove the "fact of the matter stated" issue on an individual, common law basis. Same thing applies to private gun makers and those who possess medicinal marijuana. Be aware of how you "answer" memorandums, even for informational purposes, they are tacit admissions to the jurisdiction of agency rules and procedures.

An "affirmative defense" must be pleaded at Fed.R.Civil P. 8 [c], if you are into federal procedure. I prefer the Law at Article III, and "without prejudice" UCC 1-207, where the code, whatever its charter, must be read in harmony with the Common Law at UCC 1-103.6. Uniform Commercial Code is the verbiage of the beast, least We Thee People forget, and agency is bound by it to the Constitution. "Without prejudice" is international and an ancient contract protection devise.

We are "made liable" also, after we receive a presentment and do not answer properly. Presentment is an official demand for money in payment, for a tax return not filed for a given year, or demanding we refrain from doing or to do something. This is a presumptuous instrument and must be rebutted or the unit will stand as fact when the executor goes forward with "delegation order," because we ignore the unit. Even when we do not file, we receive these notices and an answer must be forthcoming, although we feel put upon. All presentments must be answered quickly or you "dishonor" the negotiable unit and collection is immanent or action will be taken. Land grabs by government are ripe with "notice" of due process, especially in Hawaii. If you do not answer properly with all Rights reserved, land, taxes, summons and other notices are put into effect. It's all in the language of compliance or "tacit" non-compliance. Doing nothing will also allow agency access to your sovereign status. Remember justice is both blind and being mugged constitutionally.

All sworn personnel are federal in character and must follow Territorial Law, those who violate your state Rights are subject to "color of law" statutes because we are protected state Citizens "within" our own personam jurisdiction. Artificial citizens hath not personam at Law, but in personam subjectivity.

Black's. Dishonor; "To refuse to accept or pay a draft or to pay a promissory note when duly presented, an instrument is dishonored when a necessary or optional presentment is duly made and due acceptance or payment is refused."

"Duly presented" does not mean duly owed, is presumptive and must be rebutted or it will stand as fact of non-compliance and dishonor. The W-4 is a promissory note, which you present to the IRS via employment contract, which signed "unconditionally" will support the promise to pay accordingly and proof of contract and jurisdiction is upon the administrative record before the tribunal. Subject matter is the only issue to resolve and a judge will summarily find you guilty of the contractual infraction. If you do not pay, the instrument is "dishonored" and notices of lien, 30-day, 60-day notice will terrorize you into compliance via Article I and Article II/Executory with Admiralty support at police powers. All unconscionable memorandums or presentments should be signed "without prejudice" UCC 1-207 directly upon the instrument, copied with certified mail, dated and signed. Agency is then faced with proving their presumption of jurisdiction of the non-corporate citizen. The rebuttal becomes a fact of "notice" and agency is estoppel. All matters that can be settled at the administrative level cannot proceed to a court action for remedy. Remedy is supplied with the reservation of Rights as above stated.

WHERE

WHERE does the "made liable" emanate from? Article I/Legislative "implied power" gives the IRS presumptive power to subjugate federal citizens and corporations only, the rest of us sign in ignorance and fear, for police power of Admiralty is apparent. Title 26 is not Law for the states except where "subjects" are found within, per the 14th Amendment. All soldiers or sworn persons, government workers and subjects of corporate are under the jurisdiction of statute. We "make" ourselves liable by contracting the W-4 and most other "units" of negotiable promise improperly by waiver. If Paul of Tarsus had signed a waiver of his Rights, he would have been summarily scourged.

The 16th Amendment was not properly ratified, but remains effective for U. S. Citizens only. It did not repeal the language of the Constitution, which forbids such taxation without "representation" to the state Citizen. If those "made liable" refuted the presumption with a reservation of rights, there would not be controversy.

Article II Executive/Admiralty brain trust, puts together the blue smoke and mirrors necessary to fool most of the people all the time and your local IRS, Department of Motor Vehicles, ferret killers, bank and insurance companys do the collection on the negotiable instrument devised for its "subjects". A person who makes guns, dispenses medical marijuana, or caught with a ferret are subject to their own ignorance if threatened with an "information" or memorandum which would threaten license or possession of non-criminal property.

Statute falls when it interferes with the Bill of Rights. All We Thee People need to do is remember two words and a few numbers to reserve all our Rights. When written on the driver's license, the reservation serves notice immediately; your Rights are in effect. Do not attempt to advise sworn personnel of federal or state court what the words mean for they do not care, nor are they aware. Just sign the instrument without prejudice UCC 1-207 and cooperate. The "Truth virus" has started its work and the court is without jurisdiction to proceed because personam Remedy has been made available, unless you open your mouth and make yourself in personam to the magistrate at Rule12(b), if you go that far. You must have committed an act of criminal intent, property damage or harmed another natural person and even then you have a Right to an Article III court and jury. The People of a state cannot be a victim unless you have infringed upon another's Rights.

SILENCE is the best defense, the Bill of Rights forbids absurdity, and an attorney fits that category because he is also an officer of the tribunal and most of their work involves victimless crimes. There will be plenty of study material available so the Sovereign Citizen may protect his ass-ets. We must have knowledge of an adversary and be as "wise as the serpent" to remain a free People.

The proper remedy to seek is at the Administrative level. Jurisdiction of Personam and subject matter must be proved on the record of the tribunal or the issue cannot proceed. All issues in controversy can be proved without resort to chancery when applied properly. A court must be competent to hear an issue of dishonor. Without proper jurisdiction, evidence and witness, the court will have no "cause" to continue. We Thee

People are in a much better position than the judge, because he realizes he can violate your rights very easily and be subject to a "color of law" action, where he will be the victim. Otherwise a judge only gives the jury facts because he possesses in personam; juries are not allowed to hear law in an Article I/Executive Admiralty court, only subject matter. This is done because Citizenship status is a Law issue and the court cannot proceed if the Citizen to the presumptive inferior court does not waive his Rights and allow jurisdiction of the Tribunal. An article III court is the only forum of personam and subject matter, where Individual Rights are protected at Law, and these are seldom, if ever summoned by "Thee People." Thee People are not considered in corporate terms by statute, we subjugate ourselves per unconditional contract to assent to Civil Liberties instead of Bill of Rights. The State of California v. Ferret, is not of "The People" of Article III, but corporate at Article I and confiscation is Admiralty at negotiable unit.

Truth of Liberty is freedom and exemption from extraneous control as within Thee Bill of Rights. The 14th Amendments due process is imposed by statute law, which are civil and corporate rights of artificial citizens. We Thee People have been reduced to revenue subjects, domesticated license and contracts of Maritime 14th Amendment.

Black's. Political question. Questions of which courts will refuse to take cognizance, or to decide, on account of their purely political character, or because their determination would involve and encroachment upon the executive or legislative powers. "A matter of dispute which can be handled more appropriately by another branch of the government is not a "justifiable" matter for the courts." Baker v. Carr, 399 U.S. 186, 208-210, 82 S.Ct. 691, 705-706, 7 L.Ed.2d 663.

Your Bill of Rights becomes a very hot political question when your rights thereto have not been waived or obligated to contract. An Article I court cannot try a Sovereign Citizen, IF he has "qualified" his Citizenship status. These enumerated issues have already been decided and would be considered settled and an "absurdity" for a chancellery to hear. Such issue would not be within the preview of the Legislative/Article I inferior court, because the Supreme Court at Article III can be called to overrule any incompetent ruling of these presumptuous tribunals. Constitutional issues can totally destroy all or part of any statue that attempts to harm a Sovereign Citizen. An example, the IRS cannot answer any of Thee Peoples exemption claims unless they have a "satisfaction and accord."

I, to date have not received an answer, neither has any of the small flock of Patriots who follow this material. Article I has no civil business with the state Citizen who has protected their Rights properly. The Article I Section 8 Clause 17 U. S. Citizen is heard in an "inferior court," and Thee Sovereign Citizen has the Supreme Court as original jurisdiction at Article III. This protection and non-assumpsit of contract is so easy to use that your children can be taught to protect themselves without parental support. This is the way it was originally intended, but the seduction Spirit has adulterated the Peoples laws, which are meant for Thee Sovereign Citizen and turned our Law into an almost unrecognizable, subjugated "domestic war" that assigns us all with corporate contract, even at "corporate" birth certificate. Statue is not binding to the

American Sovereign People unless we assent. The subject citizen is bound thereby to uphold federalist sovereignty at the 14th Amendment and police power attachment. The citizenship of a subject is possession in personam at the hands of their master, Legislative Congress/Admiralty, as my Personam Citizenship is at Thee Hands of my Master, God.

A Common Law court must hear both fact and Law or you are in the wrong jurisdiction. Let not man tell you your Rights, You Stand as God intended, with your family, and counsel those "who will hear" the message of Truth.

WHY

WHY are we "made liable" and subject? Stuck on stupid, sittin on silly and waitin on dumb. We in good faith trust our government agency programs to protect US. The ignorance of this deception is enormous. We are made liable out of ignorance of who we are and volunteer in personam to signature unconditional contracts of Maritime jurisdiction.

Article 1, Section 8, Clause 1; "The Congress shall have Power to lay and collect Taxes, Duties, Impost and excises, to pay the Debts and provide for the common Defense and general Welfare of the united States; but all duties, Impost and Excises shall be uniform throughout the united States."

The above duties of Congress are enumerated for its "subjects" jurisdiction for police power and must rely upon Maritime contract. "Common defense and welfare" does not mean "profiling" and arrest for a suspicion of guilt. Neither does it contemplate "a person of interest." Taxes may be uniform for "subject persons," but the IRS admits to a "graduated" direct tax upon "persons made liable." IRS does not care who volunteers, state Citizens are more than welcome because mandate to tax is given freely and those who oppose its rules are also welcome to gather as many "persons" as possible for protest. IRS changes facts with Executive order and continues to function. You volunteer at the signing, you may also un volunteer at the signing by adding a condition to the unit.

By signing the "meeting of the minds" contract at UCC 3-104.1, "unconditionally" at UCC 3-104.2 we agree to the terms of the Congressional Article I "Penumbra Doctrine" and engraft "system" by "promise" within UCC 3-104.3 and are consequently "made liable" to "public policy" on a voluntary basis. "Without prejudice" UCC 1-207 is a "condition" of negotiability and "cannot sustain a promise" and the "executor" is "notified under penalty of perjury" of your exemption by terms of the contract, which are now constitutionally protected. All signatures, Rights and reservations thereof are on the administrative record and the trier of fact will be actionable if he bars your Rights.

The federalist use the Commerce Clause at Article I Section 8 Clause 5 as subterfuge to Thee Bill of Rights and gives "persons" civil liberties to redress. A court will not certify an unconscionable contract at UCC 2-302. The following two words also vitiate perjury, "Without Prejudice" UCC 1-207. The Uniform Commercial Code is We Thee Peoples Grace at protective advocacy with the "wolf" of agency. Few words are needed if we protect our Rights with this phrase. It simply means, "No rights are thereby waived" or "I cannot be compelled to sign an agreement of unknown benefit unless I knowingly, willingly, and intentionally assent."

No deception or engagement by agency is further tolerated at Law; to persuade us further would be actionable. We Thee People can sue the individual agent who dares go beyond his chartered codes of procedure, because then and only then can a Sovereign Citizens Rights be violated and Title 18 will issue action against the offending party. A judge would not dare step from his ministerial duty to provoke such a response from Thee People. The reason for this, you hold your personal covenant, contractual inheritance and your "personam" jurisdiction within your "right hand" and the court cannot and will not go beyond its "competent" authority of required witness, victim or criminal intent to violate his sacred Trust to his master, Article II and Congress. Only an Article III Court of Judiciary can hear your case and by not waiving your Rights, you have called upon that Power. Remember always, you are a state Citizen with status and the Law must respect and protect your Rights.

Artificial Citizens are of the 14th Amendment protective due process, you want none of it, nor will you want an attorney to "stand in your stead." An attorney, as does an "answer" to the "inferior" court in filing, admits to the jurisdiction of the tribunal, which will accept your "personam" as assent or "tacit" in personam and this you must avoid, at all cost.

Welfare clause per Black's 5th; "Constitutional provision (Art. I, Sec, 8) permitting the federal government to enact laws for the overall general welfare of the people. It is the basis for the exercise of implied powers necessary to carry out the express provisions of the Constitution."

The implied powers of "Penumbra" and "engraft" are the rebuttable presumptions that confuse We Thee People, because we take de facto laws for state Citizens as truth. Article III, only comes into play when a Sovereign state Citizen asked for their Bill of Rights. Those who are successful in not waiving their rights at contract are fortunate and will prosper. Those who do not refute the age old question of "do you understand the charges" in a court of chancery, have in "tacit" agreed to tribunal jurisdiction, when the "answer" yes, spouts the ignorance of their political values and Citizenship status. If we do not respond properly, we are bound by the presumption that we need agency to care for our daily needs and "tacit" admission that the court has the right to proceed, by pleading for us. Most of our Rights are contracted away and we do not notice the difference, because like begets like and who is the wiser.

Within the District and Territories, this implied power is 100% enforceable because the federalist has total control over "subjects under the jurisdiction thereof," at 1-8-17 and the 14th Amendment. We Thee People are safe as long as we keep our right hand closed and our personam remains intact. Federal citizens have not personam, because they owe their Citizenship and sovereignty to the government as their artificial "maker." Their citizenship and allegiance is as a soldier, at contracted residence of US Citizenship, with "subject matter" jurisdiction being the only applicable "remedy" and jurisdictional challenge. A soldier has not the personam of character per contract, nor does the corporation.

Facts of subject matter presume you were AWOL and it is up to the soldier to rebut. If asked, "do you understand the charges," by a magistrate, the only proper response I can think of is "NO" "Without Prejudice" under Uniform Commercial Code 1-207, I wish to remain silent." A judge would be stepping on Holy Ground even if he asked you what the phrase means. Even if he talks you out of the statement and into a "not so guarded" response, he would be reversed. The only other statement I would make is, "due to mistakes in fact and law, I am without competent counsel and wish to remain silent, without prejudice UCC 1-207." The objective is to get out of the Article I "inferior" court with your personam intact. The court cannot proceed without personam and subject matter jurisdiction. The "no" also puts a wrinkle in the proceeding because if you do not understand the charges, they cannot be applied to you, because you have rebutted the presumption of acceptance of them via your citizenship or Lawful status. An artificial citizen may be charged with these codes and must comply by "procedural due process" when "answer" is demanded.

HOW

HOW are We Thee People "made liable?" We sign "unconditional" contracts without "representative" signature and thereby fail to protect ourselves from avoidable controversy. Knowledge is the key, not the fancy dance of false agency teaching. Agency instruments are serious at protecting their contracted rights and the "wolf" in executor clothing awaits those "sheep" that are not vigilant at answer.

Black's. Internal. Relating to the interior; comprised within boundary lines; of interior concern or interest; domestic, as opposed to foreign.

If you keep a fist, and imagine everything within it is Gods, you will get the concept. 1-8-17 is the same to its creator. The boundary lines of Washington D.C., constitutes only ten square miles of control, which the federalist have exclusive jurisdiction. A statute "without" the Territory would constitute a fraud upon the Rights of the vigilant state Citizen, because Thee 10th Amendment supersede the Federal Constitutional aspect of Sovereign Citizenship Law and would not be authorized. Its Territories are enumerated as The District of Columbia, Guam, Puerto Rico, America Samoa, U.S. Virgin Islands, Trust Territory of the Pacific Islands, and Northern Mariana Islands. Per the IRS, these are the States under the jurisdiction of the U.S. Government. The inhabitants within these territories are, per Black's 6th, "Liable, subordinate, subservient, inferior…"

Black's. Unauthorized. That which is done without authority, as a signature or endorsement made without actual, implied or apparent authority and this includes a forgery. UCC 1-201.43.

The law is with us at every turn if we choose the proper direction. "Implied" agency is the most rampant of "apparent authority" and de facto Lex jurisdictions of the "inferior court" system. If we sign unconscionable contracts in personam, or admit tacit approval of same, we are perceived as volunteering to the manmade conditions. For our survival, our hand admits to contract beyond our assent at police power, due to "public policy" and convenience. Our failure to answer memorandums of "mail box policy" and presentments "dishonors" agency units and sets the executor at our door. Ignorance is conceived, as We Thee People cooperate with agency procedure, we are taught tolerance and cooperative chants.

I wish the people of the Territories the best, but they have as their Sovereign, an inferior State to that of the Natural Born state Preamble Citizen. The large "s" means corporate State. Article I/Congress makes laws to accommodate "persons" and do not reflect the Law of Sovereign Citizenry, for statutes are "without" the jurisdiction of Congressional control "within" a free state. The Brady Bill as it pertains to the individual state Citizen is an example and also the Marijuana initiatives, Right to die, Patriot Act, and ferret killers in California. Sovereign: Having supreme, rank, authority … rightful status of independence and prerogative … greatest in degree."

Everything within your fist is Gods; open it to sign a contract and the world will flood in personam possession. A government, which successfully takes away the individuals proper Citizenship status, is then able to assault that individual's character with "social engineering" and educational ingrain. This is how We Thee People have become domesticated within the "corporate culture" as United States Citizens.

We Thee People are of prophesy and destined to make the difference in these end times. We have a job to do and now is the time to act like WHO we are and WHO our Sovereign representative is. A government, which is not of Thee People, cannot amend or properly teach its Law. The History of a Nation is only educational and has no value beyond its merit as a knowledge tool at our base. Base knowledge is our rock and God has given us the burden to understand the political building blocks of our individual character and maintains Law of "intercourse" with mankind. Only then will love of our fellow survive us with posterity, or the corporate seduction spirit will deprive and predate our children's future.

The Dred Scott "decision," Jim Crow Laws, Civil Rights/Liberties and the 14th Amendment exist as examples of our being unfaithful to the God of this Nation by allowing its People to be subjugated and our punishment will be cast upon us through the actions of in personam ignorance.

Black's. Internal Revenue Service is responsible for administration and enforcing the internal revenue laws, except those relating to alcohol, tobacco, firearms, explosives, and wagering.

Internal, means within the governmental sovereignty jurisdiction, by Title 26 statutes of its "subjects." "EXCEPT" means within Title 27 tax jurisdiction over alcohol, tobacco, firearms, explosives, and wagering "within" your Sovereign state and by contract only. These items are 100% legally taxed within our respective state and are not voluntary.

We Thee People must give to Caesar what is Caesar's, not whatever he asked for. If you are involved with the SALE of any of these items you may be taxed 100%, IF you are within the jurisdiction and subject to the corporate statute. For instance, the income tax on Sovereign Citizens of these united States is omitted as law for it is a voluntary function authorized by "public policy" statute.

The Brady Bill and subsequent gun Laws do not apply to the natural born when buying "without" the jurisdiction of licensed gun shops where "stamps" and information are required for subjects of statute. Gun shows, ferrets, yard sales, marijuana cooperatives, income tax, etc., are not mentioned and DO NOT APPLY to the Sovereign state, but do apply within the federal jurisdictions mentioned. The state jumps in with contractual treaty type "Penumbra" to claim a partner's share of the revenue and taxes its "subject citizens" accordingly. Soldiers, bankers, IRS agents, and ferret killers are such subjects and appropriate taxes apply. No wonder they insist on the Sovereign Citizen being subjugated, if they have to pay tribute it is easier to convince others. This can be done to creatures of a State who contract as corporate entities, such as municipalities, schools, roads, post offices, 1040s, libraries and other National Citizens who seek "due process of law" per the 14th Amendment.

ONLY, when we ask permission, does the governmental mammon sovereign accept us and does so for we admit the jurisdiction and volunteer. If we do not have the knowledge to rebut or stand alone as a Sovereign Citizen with our Jesus as intercede, We Thee People will loose the redress of the First Amendment to due process of the 14th Amendment. If you have "sovereign Covenant," you will need to read slowly, and have a good Law Dictionary and Bible handy to have knowledge of these Treatises, for you are a part of The First Amendment Study Team.

We Thee People give up jurisdiction of our personam and Bill of Rights and admit to "understanding the charges" whether by "tacit" or domestication process in court or by "dishonoring a presentment." When we open our fist to predation and accept the dark master, inferior to our Natural Law, Article I presumptive and the inferior court of the IRS will apply, as opposed to Article III Judiciary, of which Thee Supreme Court has "original jurisdiction" and is looked upon by God as his intercede for our inheritance.

HOW do We Thee People avoid this "engrafted" "Penumbra Doctrine" cartel called the IRS and its police power? All you had to do was ask. The best way I have found to get along with agency is to do as they say, well almost. Keep in mind that all documents are negotiable in one form or another. I like the form that makes the document non-assumpsit and "dead in law." A contract is not negotiable if a condition is affixed "on the face of it." Prima facie evidence is the best kind and cannot be disputed when "without prejudice" UCC 1-207 is written above your signature on any unconscionable contract you sign, and it is the first thing the tribunal sees at bar and affords the trier of fact affirmative "notice." A proper reservation of Rights will not "sustain a promise," or perjury as found in Thee "Without Prejudice" treaties. Facts, which are "within" the instrument, do not apply to you if you stay "without" its terms.

Personam is your individual close and created Right of God to work as Covenant to His Law. A contract signing waives your right to divine intercede if you commit yourself to it, or allow assent to agency mischief and police power. These facts of in personam are the meat of IRS and other agency intimidation and "mail box policy," of which now we know to rebut. If you do not sign knowingly, willingly, and intentionally you cannot be held to the letter of the agreement unless there is an "accord and satisfaction." A simple rental agreement would be accord and satisfaction, when all parties are happy and nothing is forced or unconscionable at the signing. The W-4 is an opportunity to put at end this beast before it gets the "unconditional promise" it needs to survive, and "Remedy" is Thee Law Staff that will scourge the old Dragon.

Thee Truth is sometimes covered with the cloak of Law. When a situation occurs, and your Generalship is called upon, look at the contract. Revoke signatures so you can enter the issue with "clean hands" or abate its action. If there is no contract, or even if there is, sign the document before you "without prejudice" UCC 1-207 and mail it back dated and signed certified mail. Put this directly upon the presentment, for it winds up on your administrative record which is brought forward by agency.

If agency contacts you again write; "I hereby refute the validity of your unattested presentment "without dishonor," I do not owe this money," without prejudice UCC1-207. OR, "I hereby refute the validity of your unattested claim, without dishonor, I am not "made liable."

It takes agency a couple of letters for them to look up what you are saying, but one thing is certain, nothing can go to court unless the Administrative Record is clear of controversy. Attorneys are the worst of the lot in understanding this material, because there is no fight unless they can get you to change your stand. If the IRS terror machine can be estoppel, then anything is possible.

Chapter 6: Without Prejudice UCC 1-207

Black's. Without prejudice. Where an offer or admission is made "without prejudice," or a motion is denied or a suit dismissed "without prejudice," it is meant as a declaration that no rights or privileges of the party concerned are to be considered as thereby waived or lost accept in so far as may be expressly conceded or decided.

A signing of "without prejudice" entitles the Sovereign Citizen to Thee Bill of Rights, which attach to his person or "personam" and those rights are not waived unless through actions on the part of the sovereign at a future date or a court decision in advance of your reservation. Your political knowledge must defend your contracting needs and all controversies must be settled with written correspondence. You're right to avoid consequences of statute or commercially assigned obligations put the burden on plaintiff to prove his statements with verified or sworn instruments.

Agency police power is voided upon notice of the "personam" Citizen. "Probable cause" rather than civil statute of "reasonable cause" is required. "Artificial" "persons" who obligate to the subject matter instrument are "made liable" to its delict. An "unconditional" signing gives the agency court in personam and subject matter jurisdiction per Rule 12(b). Without prejudice reserves your personam and takes away the "inferior" court requirement, of having both subject matter and in personam jurisdiction. The Article I court cannot judge an action until it clears the administrative level and has acquired both jurisdictions. Article III Judicial must try sovereign citizens by design, after criminal intent has been alleged.

Uniform Commercial Code 1-207. "Performance or Acceptance Under Reservation of Rights. (1) A party who with explicit reservation of rights performs or promises performance or assents to performance in a manner demanded or offered by the other party does not thereby prejudice the rights reserved. Such words as "without prejudice," "under protest" or the like are sufficient."

A reservation of Thee Bill of Rights is a demand and notice, which gives We Thee People our proper status as state citizens and a court of Article III Law.

Amendment VII: "In Suits at common Law, where the controversy shall exceed twenty dollars, the right of trial by jury shall be preserved, and no fact tried by jury, shall be otherwise re-examined in any Court of the united States, than according to the rules of the common law."

A sovereign Citizen cannot be tried in a statutory inferior court without his consent and your contracting without a reservation of rights ensures disaster of political status. The use of the UCC is for those contracts, which are commercially forced upon the Sovereign Citizen and are essential for proper remedy at Law. The W-4, drivers license, bank, school and agency protective services are the presumptive contractual systems and these are "engraft" of "Penumbra Doctrine" and the "implied powers" of Article I and Article II, which "makes" Admiralty, and puts you before the "inferior" courts with the burden of proving innocence. Penalties of perjury are of criminal intent and must be protected or the adversity of the issue will apply via your waiver.

Black's. An accord being a contract, the requirements of mutual assent and consideration must be met. Buob v. Feenaughty Machinery Co., 191 Wash. 477, 71 P.2d 559, 564.

A contract signed under duress is unconscionable and must be represented "without prejudice" or the instrument is treated as "satisfaction and accord" before the trier of fact.

Black's. Unconcionability. Unconcionability is generally recognized to include an absence of meaningful choice on the part of one of the parties, to a contract together with contract terms, which are unreasonably favorable to the other party. Gordon v. Crown Central Petroleum Corp., D.C.Ga., 423 F.Supp. 58, 61.

Procedural advantages are granted to the executor, which allows facts agreed upon to be carried out, even police power of court. The only reason I signed a W-4 was to engrave without prejudice upon it. My job requires the W-4 form and the reservation brings peace to the issue of being exempt. Without the reservation, I would have been assessed a $500 frivolous penalty. My employer and the IRS are contracted entities and I do not wish to participate or "benefit" with them.

Remember, the perjury portion is a statute criminal matter. Once into the body of the contract, all corporate rights are protected and wiggling the facts are forbidden. The 5th Amendment cannot protect your waived rights, for court decisions advise the reservation must be made upon the instrument as a clear indicator of your intention. Your voluntary act of signature without your representation is your cause of worry. Since there is no place in the 1040 to put a claim for defense, the Citizen must write their objections upon the "unit" or prima facie. The "Privacy Act" states that when a person is "made liable;" they are required to send a "return or tax statement." A reservation of rights breaks this "made liable" into Constitutional issues that the IRS cannot deal with.

Black's. Uniform Commercial Code. (1) If the court as a matter of law finds the contract or any clause of the contract to have been unconscionable at the time it was made the court may refuse to enforce the contract, or may enforce the remainder of the contract without the unconscionable clause or it may so limit the application of any unconscionable clause as to avoid any unconscionable result. (2) When it is claimed or appears to the court that the contract or any clause thereof may be unconscionable the parties shall be afforded a reasonable opportunity to present evidence as to its commercial setting, purpose and effect to aid the court in making the determination.

UCC Section 2-302 should be construed in conjunction with the obligation of good faith imposed at several places in the Code. See UCC 1-203.

A contract cannot be forced upon the Sovereign Citizen, and when faced with no way out; the vigilant must reserve their rights. All signings are voluntary and lawful, but the Sovereign cannot allow "good faith" alone to guide our political knowledge. When in doubt protect yourself at all times. We Thee People must "bind the hands of government to the constitution to prevent mischief;" words of Thomas Jefferson are the warnings of Thee founding fathers. The mischief We Thee People suffer comes as assumpsit.

Black's. Assumpsit. He undertook: he promised. A promise or engagement by which one person assumes or undertakes to do some act or pay something to another. It may be either oral or in writing, but is not under seal. It is express if the promisor puts his engagement in distinct and definite language; it is implied where the law infers a promise (though no formal one has passed) from the conduct of the party or the circumstances of the case. Duke v. Rogers, 67 Ga.App. 661, 21 S.E.2d 295, 297.

The law "infers" a promise when it gives a child a social security card at birth. When the conduct of the child has moved them out into the real world, their application to the system is "express." When the paperwork is signed, your child will toil as you have in this Promised Land. We Thee People must reserve our children's rights from birth, and at their school.

Black's. Unconscionable bargain. An unconscionable bargain or contract is one which no man in his senses not under delusion, would make, on the one hand, and which no fair and honest man would accept, on the other. Hume v. U.S. 406, 10 S.Ct. 134, 33 L.Ed. 393.

The IRS cannot be considered fair or honest and contracting with them only makes the sovereign Citizen fair game for tribute. A volunteer is "made liable" at the "Penumbra" "writing" of contract. Perjury is the statute of design and Admiralty, the springboard for agency mischief and police power.

Black's. Perjury. In criminal law, the willful assertion as to a matter of fact, opinion belief, or knowledge, made by a witness in a judicial proceeding as part of his evidence, either under oath or in any form allowed by law to be substituted for an oath whether such evidence is given in open court, or in an affidavit or otherwise, such asseveration being material to the issue or point of inquiry and known to such witness to be false. Gatewood v. State, 15 Md.App. 314, 290 A.2d 551, 553.

I cannot think of any contract a Citizen may sign, which may bring perjury when you the "entitled" Citizen protect their Rights.

Black's. False. The word "false" has two distinct and well-recognized meanings: (1) intentionally or knowingly or negligently untrue, (2) untrue by mistake or accident, or honestly after the exercise of reasonable care. Metropolitan Life Ins. Co. v. Adams, D.C.Mun.App.,37 A.2d 345, 350.

You can see that it does not take much to sign an instrument incorrectly, and be fined by agency without proof of being guilty. The difference is obvious only in the "writing." Once you are inside the body of the W-4 and have agreed to the amount of deductions and terms "unconditionally," the waiver takes place because the unit has been "executed." Without prejudice does not allow the "execution" of a contract and reserves your rights. Your reservation also puts a condition on the unit, vitiates its perjury and summary procedure which makes the unit non-negotiable and "dead in law."

Black's. Negotiable instruments. To be negotiable within the meaning of U.C.C. Article 3, an instrument must meet the requirements set out in Section 3-104: (1) it must be writing signed by the maker or drawer.

The W-4 unit is required to be signed and delivered to sworn persons of Executive Branch Departments "Penumbra" HEAD. An agent representing the IRS is usually the person who assigns you these instruments. These are usually employees who work for the chartered corporation that you rub elbows with at work. That particular "employee" has the job of giving you all the paperwork possible to get you on board this Admiralty fleet of ignorance and is from the personnel department. This not so innocent W-4 unit will "engraft" with other required instruments of one type or the other as clarified in the "Penumbra Doctrine" and created de facto police power.

The marriage between Article I and Article II is a convenience for the sovereign citizen because of the Separation of Powers. The W-4 is the vilest of the "implied power" forms. To be separate and not joined at the Flag, Congress at Article I nor Admiralty at Article II combined, can interfere with Article I Section 2 Clause 3; "Representatives and direct taxes shall be apportioned." There is not a soul around who can help you with the mystery. WHY? Why am I required to sign an agreement that I know only an ignorant fool would agree to while intoxicated? Unconscionable, you can bet your next "stripe" on it soldier!

The unit is now executed and ready for your tribute. You had no opportunity to negotiate and the agent and the employer will take the "penumbra" share back to its creator, U.S. Treasury. Admiralty is the muscle of the President and "forums" of procedural facts will dance before you and attract your attention to the body of the now negotiable unit. A meeting of the minds has transformed a sovereign state Citizen into "domesticated product", and "artificial persons" of Article I Section 8 Clause 17, as a United States Citizens, and you are now "subject" to the direct tax.

Negotiable Instrument further states; "it must contain an UCC 3-104(2) unconditional UCC3-104(3) promise or order.

Without Prejudice UCC 1-207 above your signature not only puts a condition on an unconditional contract, but also reserves all your rights under Article III Judicial. Police power is void unless "crime" and probable cause exist.

I think this odd, coming from Congress at Article I, but I am grateful to God for His Grace, because this appears to be the only way to reserve our freedom without contest. The W-4 is not viable unless you wish to have the agent deduct your social security. My next job will be to exclude a social security number on the same "reserved" unit. Employers have no power over the use of the W-4 by the Citizen. The IRS takes care of those who wonder from their flock, if they have charter to hold them.

We Thee People have the right to contract or not, and cannot be forced to sign any instrument, when we do so for convenience and peace lets all protect ourselves. Our individual personam will make us very powerful as a state and posterity with the family of man will return.

"An unconstitutional statute, though having the form of law, is in reality, no law and imposed no duties, confers no rights, creates no office, bestows no power on anyone and justifies no actions performed under it." Am. Jur. 2d Sec. 256.

The graduated income tax is unconstitutional only, if the citizen abates its "color of law," "without Prejudice" to him.

Bouvier's 1914 Law Encyclopedia. "It must be permitted of men to buy his peace without prejudice to them." "It has been held that one may buy his peace by compromising a claim which he knows is without right." Daily v. King, 70 Mich. 568, 44 N.W. 959, "but the compromise of an illegal claim will not sustain a promise." Read v. Hitchings, 71 ME 590.

A police officer will have pen hand as well as the weapons of war because he must protect himself from the corporate Citizens who have given him the police power. All instruments you sign will lead to your political destruction if you do not protect your Bill of Rights at this stage. This is very important for it brings the Judiciary of Article III into play at probable. UCC 1-103.6 states "The Code cannot be read to preclude a Common Law action."

Without Prejudice serves notice upon any agent, that you are not waiving any of your state Bill of Rights. Beware of agency procedure and sign everything with Thee reservation to make the instrument non-assumpsit.

Black's. Non-assumpsit. The general issue in the action of assumpsit; being a plea by which the defendant avers, "he did not partake" or promise as alleged.

When We Thee People are put in a circumstance of compromise, the only viable solution this scribe has found relies on Thee Uniform Commercial Code and its direct link to Thee Constitution of these united States of America.

"But whenever the Judicial Power is called into play. It is responsible to the fundamental law and no other authority can intervene to force or authorize the judicial body to disregard it." Yakus v. U.S 321 U.S. 414 pg. 468 (1944).

The officer may not know the Law and will probably proceed with whatever "forum" is to be taken per his training instructions. He is a "ministerial" officer of the court and is given very little discretional knowledge. When our Rights are violated by agency, we must cooperate with constitutional recourse and remedy. The agents must sign forms also and these become permanent record of the administrative process that will receive your judicial notice.

Our state citizenship is brought forth along with our personam Rights, which do not mingle well with statute procedure. A court appearance would be to gain jurisdiction over your personam. I would suggest that for study purposes you answer politely, that you do not understand the charges, and "without prejudice" under Uniform Commercial Code 1-207, "due to mistakes in fact and Law, I wish to remain silent."

The magistrate will have to be very constructive in his "color of law" procedure because his boundaries to engage you further are abated. Without contract or tacit admission to the jurisdiction, it is finished. Remember, you are in an Article I "inferior" court, brought by Admiralty and the only power this court has over the sovereign Citizen is to give Remedy or take the issue to the Grand Jury for indictment under Article III if there is criminal intent. The 5th Amendment states; "No person shall be held to answer for a capitol or otherwise infamous crime, unless on presentment of a Grand Jury." If there is no victim and criminal intent, there is no crime.

"It may however, be considered settled that letters or admissions containing the expression in substance that they are to be "without prejudice" will not be admitted in evidence … an arrangement stating the letter was without prejudice was held to be inadmissible as evidence … not only will the letter bearing the words, "without prejudice" but also the answer thereto, which was not so guarded, was inadmissible." Ferry v. Taylor, 33 Mo. 323; Durgin v. Somers, 117 Mass 55, Molyneaux v. Collier, 13 Ga. 406. When correspondence had commenced "without prejudice" but afterwards those words were dropped, it was immaterial, 6 Ont. 719.

Without Prejudice UCC 1-207, above your signature, on an instrument will represent the following:

Not a promise to appear and vitiates perjury.
Enforces the Right to contract and the right to compromise an unconscionable contract.
Reserves all applicable Bill of Rights and Article III judicial Power.
"Criminal intent" must be brought forward to proceed.
Separation of Powers.
All Constitutional terms dealing with contracts, judicial and taxes.
Reserves "personam" jurisdictional issues.
Estoppel of subject matter only jurisdiction, and summary Admiralty.
Non-assumpsit.
Habeas Corpus.

Activating clause for police power at "probable cause."
Disrupts Penumbra Doctrine.
(13) Confession and avoidance.

Miranda will be given for you to sign, reserve your rights on this instrument by not becoming in personam at Rule 12 (b). Do not give up your personam to "power of attorney" because you waive rights with each admission or tacit response answered by "persons standing in your stead," which makes you in personam for accepting this "benefit." Remain SILENT and the reservation will command you to Justice.

God Bless!

ABOUT THE AUTHOR

The author is from a small southern Christian Community where contracts were spoken aloud and hands were shaken in fellowship. Word is bond and few would dare transgress upon an agreement. This love of our Brother has been reduces to 'summary' contract.

The author failed the second grade in Louisiana and averaged out in several California High Schools. He did not get interested in any meaningful study until he attended college. He found a Constitutional Law class which taught Lawyers how to make elliptical, everyday words to mean whatever they presumed. He decided there was more to Law than "social engineering" and being a Reserve Deputy Sheriff.

He became an insurance agent in Tennessee and soon learned that he was up to his neck in Lawyers and Bankers. He decided to fall back on his limited resources and fled back to California. He is a self studied Administrative Law Consultant whom has found that words within the Bill of Rights are of God's Law.